# THE MINISTRY OF HEALING

## Dr. Ernest S. Martin

# CONTENTS

This manuscript is a portion of sermons on healing preached by Dr. Ernest S. Martin D.V.M.

Thanks to Christine Miller for typing the taped sermons.

I would like to thank my wife, Jan, and son, James, for all their work getting this book edited and published.

Scripture passages are New King James Version of the Bible. Published by E. S. Martin Publishing, April 2013.

Revised July 2022.

# INTRODUCTION

When healing is discussed, all kinds of beliefs are raised. Some people believe that God does not heal today. Others think that God can heal if he wants to. Some believe that he will heal if it is his will. And still others have the extreme view that God will heal if one just asks. Thus we need to turn to God's Word for answers as to what God does say about healing. Examples of healing in the Old Testament will be presented as well as what the Word says about illness. The New Testament describes many occasions when Jesus healed someone as well as the healings performed by the apostles. The seven types of illnesses presented will help believers understand and pray for healing today.

These types of illnesses are:

1. Curse and Rebellion
2. Illness unto Death
3. For the Glory of God
4. Chastisement Caused by Sin
5. Demonic Afflictions
6. Abusing Our Bodies
7. Molding of the Spirit

# BEING PREPARED FOR JESUS'S POWER

Jesus sent the twelve disciples to preach the good news, and he sent them with the power to heal the sick and cast out devils. As we progress, we will see how Jesus did this. Mark 3:13–15 says:

And he goeth up into a mountain, and calleth unto him whom he would: and they came unto him. And he ordained twelve, that they should be with him, and that he might send them forth to preach, and to have power to heal sicknesses, and to cast out devils.

Luke 9:1–3 says:

Then he called his twelve disciples together, and gave them power and authority over all devils, and to cure diseases. And he sent them to preach the kingdom of God, and to heal the sick. And he said unto them, Take nothing for your journey, neither staves, nor scrip, neither bread, neither money; neither have two coats apiece.

If we know that we are doing the work of the Father and being led by the Spirit, then we can go with the confidence that we have the authority to cast out demons and heal the sick. The key is learning to know the will of God and the mind of Christ. Through this lesson series, I am going to provide some tools that hopefully will allow us to learn to walk with this authority.

1

Luke 10:1–2 says:

> After these things the Lord appointed other seventy also, and sent them two and two before his face into every city and place, whither he himself would come. Therefore said he unto them, The harvest truly is great, but the laborers are few: pray ye therefore the Lord of the harvest, that he would send forth laborers into his harvest.

We see in the above passage that Jesus sent them by twos. He did this not because there is comfort in numbers but because the law requires the mouth of two witnesses. As the Lord sent out the witnesses, he asked that they not get jealous and want to be the only ones but to pray for more laborers. He also said to rejoice for someone who led a person to Christ, even if that person who accepted Christ was someone for whom you had labored.

The last statement reminds me of an evangelist's testimony that I heard. He said that once when he was traveling from church-to-church, preaching, he was asked to pray for a parishioner who was not saved, even though he had been attending church regularly for forty years. One night, after the evangelist preached his message, the man came forward and accepted Christ as his personal Savior. The evangelist was elated to see that the man had come forward. He asked the man exactly what in his message led the man to come forward.

He replied, "Preacher, I don't really know what you said. I have been watching my dear precious wife for forty years who has put up with me. I simply could not take it anymore. I had to turn my life over to Christ."

The evangelist rejoiced. He knew that it was not important as to "who" led this man to accept Christ, but the fact that he accepted Christ was cause for rejoicing.

Luke 10:3–20 says:

> Go your ways: behold, I send you forth as lambs among wolves. Carry neither purse, nor scrip, nor shoes: and salute no man by the way. And into whatsoever house ye enter, first say, Peace be to this house. And if the son of peace be there, your

peace shall rest upon it: if not, it shall turn to you again. And in the same house remain, eating and drinking such things as they give: for the laborer is worthy of his hire. Go not from house to house. And into whatsoever city ye enter, and they receive you, eat such things as are set before you: and heal the sick that are therein, and say unto them, The kingdom of God is come nigh unto you. But into whatsoever city ye enter, and they receive you not, go your ways out into the streets of the same, and say, Even the very dust of your city, which cleaveth on us, we do wipe off against you: notwithstanding, be ye sure of this, that the kingdom of God is come nigh unto you. But I say unto you, that it shall be more tolerable in that day for Sodom, Woe unto thee, Chora'zin! woe unto thee, Bethsai'da! for if the mighty works had been done in Tyre and Sidon, which have been done in you, they had a great while ago repented, sitting in sackcloth and ashes. But it shall be more tolerable for Tyre and Sidon at the judgment, than for you. And thou, Caper'na-um, which art exalted to heaven, shalt be thrust down to hell. He that heareth you heareth me; and he that despiseth you despiseth me; and he that despiseth me despiseth him that sent me. And the seventy returned again with joy, saying, Lord, even the devils are subject unto us through thy name. And he said unto them, I beheld Satan as lightning fall from heaven. Behold, I give unto you power to tread on serpents and scorpions, and over all the power of the enemy; and nothing shall by any means hurt you. Notwithstanding, in this rejoice not, that the spirits are subject unto you; but rather rejoice, because your names are written in heaven.

The Bible says to make sacrificial praise unto God. If there are times when we feel that we just really cannot praise God, then we must reflect on our salvation and thank God that our name is written in the book of life. If we do this, then we will see that once again we can praise him. Someday we will stand face-to- face with our Lord and Savior, which is paramount above all else.

When the Lord first began speaking to me about how to deal with demon powers, he did this by bringing the scriptures alive to me. As I was driving to work one day, Satan spoke to me very loudly and clearly saying, "I'm going to take everything you have away from you."

I cannot describe the fear that gripped me. I knew without a doubt that Satan meant business. For the next seventy-two hours, I went through a "living hell." At that time, we had two children; we now have four. I had my own business, and we had a house. God began to speak to me for the next three days, but he let me live in fear. I had to come to a place where I was willing to give up everything that I had, literally saying, "God, it's yours." I gave it up, starting with material things. I thought that I would lose my house and my business.

As I sorted through these feelings, my conclusion was that they were only material things and that, eventually, they would be gone anyway. I started with my house, saying, "Satan, you can have it. I can always find some place to live." Next I followed with other material things, no longer becoming attached to them. I came to the point of being able to totally surrender them. I struggled with the hard part. Could I give up my wife and children? God began to speak to me. He said, "I gave my son for you. Abraham was willing to give Isaac. Can you give your child?"

I finally concluded that, yes, I could. I did this because I knew that in the end, my children would be with God, and someday, I would see them again. Then it came to my wife. God said to me, "Can you give her up?"

Just like my children, I knew that eventually I would see her in heaven. I told myself that it would be better for her because she would not have to put up with me anymore. Therefore my reply was, "Yes, Lord, I can give her up." I totally had to surrender all.

I cannot describe the freedom that this brought me. Satan no longer had a hold on me. Fear is how Satan works. God said, "Fear not the one who can take your life but fear the one who can send you to hell." If we are going to go out and wage warfare on Satan, then we must first come to the point where we have no fear of what he can do.

I would like to share some of the dreams and a vision that God gave me, which led me into total surrender. Words cannot describe what it is like to be "totally pure," but God translated this to me through a dream. I was about thirty years old, and it was just for a moment, but it was indescribable. The Lord chooses different ways to reach different people, and I often think that he chose this way to reach me because I am so bullheaded and stubborn. I have met many people who have seen visions of Jesus, and at one time, I was envious. I wanted to see Jesus too. I pleaded and begged with God, and he said to me, "If you see Jesus momentarily with your eyes, it will fade very quickly; however, if you will open your spiritual eyes and ears then you will have Him every day through my Word."

"Lord, give it to me in the Word and open my spiritual eyes and ears so that I might know Jesus," was my reply. And he did. To prepare us for our encounters, God uses what he needs to.

I once met the high priest of the Church of Satan over the southwest district of the United States. His wife left the Church of Satan, which they expressly forbade, and I met with him to ask him for her life. He granted it. I cannot describe the power of God that was present when I was in the room with him. This man said to me, "Satan tells me very clearly that you belong to God and that I will be dealing with the Holy Spirit. Because of this, I will deal with you." He also said that he could not count the number of people who do not know God who have come to tell him things. We had a long theological discussion that lasted for about two hours. This is an example of how God prepares you when he has something that he needs for you to do. In other words, we have a God who is who he needs to be at the moment. Sometimes, in the heat of a crisis, it may seem as though he is far away, but he is not.

Acts 3:1–12 says:

> Now Peter and John went up together into the temple at the hour of prayer, being the ninth hour. And a certain man lame from his mother's womb was carried, whom they laid daily at the gate of the temple which is called Beautiful, to ask alms of them that entered into the temple; who, seeing Peter and John about to go into the temple, asked an alms. And Peter, fastening his eyes upon him with John, said, Look on us. And he gave heed unto them, expecting to receive

something of them. Then Peter said, Silver and gold have I none; but such as I have give I thee: In the name of Jesus Christ of Nazareth rise up and walk. And he took him by the right hand, and lifted him up: and immediately his feet and ankle bones received strength. And he leaping up stood, and walked, and entered with them into the temple, walking, and leaping, and praising God. And all the people saw him walking and praising God: and they knew that it was he which sat for alms at the Beautiful gate of the temple: and they were filled with wonder and amazement at that which had happened unto him. And as the lame man which was healed held Peter and John, all the people ran together unto them in the porch that is called Solomon's, greatly wondering. And when Peter saw it, he answered unto the people, Ye men of Israel, why marvel ye at this? or why look ye so earnestly on us, as though by our own power or holiness we had made this man to walk?

So often today, we hear people saying, "Come to my meeting. I will pray for you, and you will get well." Or "God has spoken to me and anointed my hands, and when I pray for you, you will get well." We should take caution when hearing this.

The apostles did not say that. Instead, they said, "Why do you look at us? It is not by our power, but the power of God that this man was healed." In other words, they were saying that any man who was led by the Spirit of God could have done the same thing.

Acts 3:13–16 says:

The God of Abraham, and of Isaac, and of Jacob, the God of our fathers, hath glorified his Son Jesus; whom ye delivered up, and denied him in the presence of Pilate, when he was determined to let him go. But ye denied the Holy One and the Just, and desired a murderer to be granted unto you; and killed the Prince of life, whom God hath raised from the dead; whereof we are witnesses. And his name, through faith in his name, hath made this man strong, whom ye see and know: yea, the faith which is by him hath given him this perfect soundness in the presence of you all.

I used to look at this occurrence as something that the Jews and Pharisees did.

Then, one day, God spoke to me and said, "You crucified My Son." I said to him, "But, Lord, I wasn't there."

"Oh yes, you were," was his reply.

Then I realized that I did crucify his Son, and he only used those people to do the work. I crucified him! I nailed him to the cross! I pushed the crown of thorns onto his brow! Once I saw this, I then was able to realize what he had done for me. Even though I did not stand at the cross before I came to Christ, my whole life crucified him.

In First Timothy, Paul says that he is the chief among the sinners. When I set myself against the standards of Jesus, I, too, am a wretched sinner beyond any description of words. Against his righteousness, my righteousness is worse than the filthy rags that the Bible talks about. When I look at him, I ask myself, "How can I condemn any other sinner?"

Paul approved the murder of Steven, and he did it in the name of God, which made it even worse. So how can I judge any other sinner since I am a sinner also? When I look at the holiness of Christ and his righteousness, I see that I cannot judge any other man because I fall so truly short of Jesus. When we look at God, we come to realize exactly where we stand.

Acts 3:17–19 says:

> And now, brethren, I wot that through ignorance ye did it, as did also your rulers. But those things, which God before had showed by the mouth of all his prophets, that Christ should suffer, he hath so fulfilled. Repent ye therefore, and be converted, that your sins may be blotted out, when the times of refreshing shall come from the presence of the Lord.

In the passage above, Peter is saying that even though the Lord was crucified, nailed to a cross and rejected, he still loves us. If we would just recognize this and repent, then we would be forgiven. What a wonderful love! What a wonderful God!

Acts 5:12–16 says:

And by the hands of the apostles were many signs and wonders wrought among the people; (and they were all with one accord in Solomon's porch. And of the rest durst no man join himself to them: but the people magnified them. And believers were the more added to the Lord, multitudes both of men and women) insomuch that they brought forth the sick into the streets, and laid them on beds and couches, that at the least the shadow of Peter passing by might overshadow some of them. There came also a multitude out of the cities round about unto Jerusalem, bringing sick folks, and them which were vexed with unclean spirits: and they were healed every one.

In John 14:12, Jesus spoke about "works," and Jesus said, "If you believe, the works that I do you shall do, and greater works because I go unto the Father." At no time did they bring people for Jesus's shadow to pass over them. We did, however, learn of people being laid in the byways so that Peter's shadow might cast over them, and they might be healed. This is an example of the "greater works" that Jesus spoke of. In the book of Acts, there is no "Amen" at the end, indicating the works continued.

I have been asked, "Why do we not see these greater works today?" I do not know the true answer to this question, but through much thought and consideration, I have devised my own ideas and theories. I have wondered if it could be that we are not really praying, looking, believing, and reaching out to God. Are we really making ourselves available to be used of him?

Mr. Smith Wigglesworth once walked down the aisle of a train, and people fell into the aisle, asking, "What must we do to be saved?" He never spoke a word to cause people to do this. He never even read the newspaper; he only read the Bible. He totally and completely gave himself to God. I look at this and think that God must be looking for people who have totally and completely given of themselves to him. The thing that concerns me is that as Christians, must we reach a point of being severely persecuted before we will finally turn ourselves over to God? Why do we wait for persecution? The first thing that God said in the book of Revelation to the church of Ephesus was that *they had lost their first love*. I ask this question to myself and to us all, "Do we love Jesus as much today as we did the first day that we were saved?" Honestly, I must say that I do not; restore unto me the joy of your salvation, my Lord.

It is natural for us to become cynical. Sometimes when we pray, and we think that our prayers are not answered. The Lord always answers our prayers, even if we do not realize it. Sometimes we are just not willing to accept the answer "No." Sometimes we are not willing to "wait" for God to do his work. If we pray for a lost person, then we want them to be saved "now," especially if it is our children. The number one problem of a parent is taking their child off the cross because they cannot bear to watch them suffer.

If you take a person off the cross too many times, then they will get to the point that nothing will work. We must let the Lord perform his works.

I once watched a man struggle for seven years to come to Christ. He knew that he was lost. He knew that he was dead in his sins. Instead of asking for a pardon, he kept looking for a technicality to get him off or to see if he could find a way to beat the law. For seven years he did this, and finally God said to him, "There is no technicality; you have used up all your appeals, so either receive me or reject me."

This is a prime example of what is happening to people today; they keep trying to find a technicality. They know the truth and they know where they are; however, they keep trying to find a way out instead of saying, "I am guilty." They do all of this instead of admitting their sins and pleading for God's mercy.

This is the same thing that is happening with our families. We find things to make it easier for them instead of just turning them over to God and saying, "You've made your bed, and now you can sleep in it." If we could only just pray to God about our loved ones and then trust God to do his works over them. The key is that the more we know God, the more we can trust him. Faith does not come because we go through a series of mental gymnastics, repeating something over and over. Faith comes when we know that we can trust God. It does not require a "boat load" of faith but only a "mustard seed" of faith, which is a very tiny amount. The bigger the God, the less faith is required. Our God is very big, so all that is required of us is to have only just a mustard seed of faith.

There are certain people in my family whom I would like to have on either side of me if I were walking down a dark alley. They would lay their life down for me, and they are big enough to protect me; however, they are midgets compared to our God.

Several years ago, a woman whose husband had broken her arm came to our house. She said that her husband had a gun and was coming to kill her. At that point, I prayed and decided to call a friend. I said to him, "We are going to go to this guy's house before he comes here."

So we did. I knocked on his door and said, "Can I come in?" He said, "My wife is at your place, isn't she?"

"Yes, sir," I replied.

He said, "You can come in, but I am leaving. I am going to your house."

I then walked in. I could see the gun sticking out from the front of his pants. He was in a rage. After walking in, we sat down. I then looked at him and said, "You are the most gutless wonder that I have ever seen in my life. You call yourself a man? No man breaks his wife's arm." I then repeated, "You are not a man, you are a gutless wonder, and I am not afraid of you. You might have that gun in your belt and you could shoot and kill this man, but you cannot kill me because my spirit lives forever with God."

Before the night was over, he laid his gun down and prayed to receive Jesus Christ. He then fell over, weeping, and said to me, "Thank God you came because I would have killed my wife tonight, and I would have killed you and your whole family for protecting her."

God's power was there with us that night. I wish I could tell you that the man was walking with God today, but he is not. The marriage was dissolved, but he did not kill her and his children, which is what he had set out to do. I tell you this story to show you how sometimes you must be prepared for what God wants you to do. This was a case where I moved the Spirit. I said to God, "I have got to do something, so I am walking, trusting that you are walking with me and going before me." We had a lot of people praying that night. I can guarantee that my wife and his wife knew exactly where I was going. They were on their knees, praying for God to protect us; and he did.

# OUT OF THE FLESH AND INTO THE SPIRIT

A cts 9:32–35 says:

> And it came to pass, as Peter passed throughout all quarters, he came down also to the saints which dwelt at Lydda. And there he found a certain man named Aene'as, which had kept his bed eight years, and was sick of the palsy. And Peter said unto him, Aene'as, Jesus Christ maketh thee whole: arise, and make thy bed. And he arose immediately. And all that dwelt at Lydda and Sharon saw him, and turned to the Lord.

We see in the passage above that Peter spoke in the name of Jesus Christ, and a man was healed.

Acts 14:8–10 says:

> And there sat a certain man at Lystra, impotent in his feet, being a cripple from his mother's womb, who never had walked: the same heard Paul speak: who steadfastly beholding him, and perceiving that he had faith to be healed, said with a loud voice, Stand upright on thy feet. And he leaped and walked.

An interesting thing that comes out in this scripture is that Paul noticed that the man had the faith to be healed. In the previous scripture, it was through Peter's faith and the Holy Spirit that God could do his work. One of the gifts of the Spirit is the gift of faith.

There are many different opinions as to how the gifts of the Spirit function. My opinion is that if you have the Holy Spirit and God needs it, any one of the gifts can function in your life. In other words, if we are available, and God needs one of the gifts to function, then it can function.

An example of this is that one night in one of our Bible studies where we were ministering primarily to drug addicts, there was a young woman who had an eye problem that doctors could not fix. She made the comment, "I would like for my eyes to be healed so that I won't go blind, but I don't have the faith."

At that very moment, the Lord spoke to me and said, "I have just given you the faith for her. Now give it to her."

I spoke to her and said, "Ann, God has just given me the faith, and I give it to you. Now receive it in Jesus's name."

She said, "I do, and hallelujah, I am healed."

It was just as when Paul saw the man and perceived that he had the faith to be healed. Paul spoke it, and the man was healed. We find that God does not operate the same way all the time. Jesus did not heal everybody the same way, the apostles did not heal everybody the same way, and in the Old Testament, the prophets did not heal everybody the same way. It is as God's Spirit moves. If we are sensitive and available, we will be there to be used of God.

Acts 19:11–12 says:

> And God wrought special miracles by the hands of Paul: so that from his body were brought unto the sick handkerchiefs or aprons, and the diseases departed from them, and the evil spirits went out of them.

It is interesting that if you study the life of Paul, you will see that Paul did not seek to be used as somebody special. He was available, he preached the Word, he was committed to God, and he listened to the Spirit. God performed many miracles through his hands, just as today God uses some people's hands. Does this mean that their hands have healing powers? No. It is only if the Spirit of God moves through them. It is not of the Lord when one says, "My hands are anointed, and if you come to me, I will lay my hands upon you and heal you." This statement glorifies a man, and God says, "No man takes my glory." If God uses you, be incredibly careful that you turn the praise back up to God. When God begins to use you, it is very humbling, but it is extremely easy for pride to step in.

Matthew 7:21–23 says:

> Not every one that saith unto me, Lord, Lord, shall enter into the kingdom of heaven; but he that doeth the will of my Father which is in heaven. Many will say to me in that day, Lord, Lord, have we not prophesied in thy name? and in thy name have cast out devils? and in thy name done many wonderful works? And then will I profess unto them, I never knew you: depart from me, ye that work iniquity.

The passage above shows us the danger of letting pride step in. God gave Paul a thorn in the flesh to protect him from self-exaltation and pride. Paul was so powerfully used that God said he would give him a messenger of Satan to buffet him but that his grace was sufficient to handle it. I do not know and would not even try to conjecture what that messenger of Satan was that buffeted Paul, however, Paul learned to appreciate it because, in his weakness, he found the strength of God. This messenger of Satan kept him humble, and he knew the importance of this. It is easy to have a problem with pride. We must keep in mind that pride comes before the fall.

I would like to share with you an occurrence that happened in my life in a parking lot in Dallas, Texas. A young man came up to me one night and said, "There is a man out here you are probably going to meet. He is my best friend. When we were in California, I got angry with him one day. I put a curse on him that would not take his life but would cause something serious to happen to him. He broke his neck on a surfboard. Now he is paralyzed."

We witnessed to this young man and talked to him. He said to us, "I have got such great power. I can heal people and bring people down. I do not want to give up this power."

I said to him, "Are you tormented?"

He said, "I am in horrible torment day and night, all of the time."

I asked him if he wanted peace, and his reply was, "I cannot give up the power."

Later that night, I met the man that was paralyzed and witnessed to him. I prayed that night that he would get no peace and get no sleep until he made peace with God. At three o'clock that morning, he called me at home and said, "I cannot sleep."

"I did not think so," I replied.

The next day, I met with him and his brother-in-law. This meeting resulted in a relationship that eventually led to establishing some ministries.

In my office one Sunday, I was talking to a young woman who said, "I didn't know that the devil was alive."

This struck me by surprise. I just did not understand how one could not know the power of Satan and his slyness and deception. Some may think that if they go to church, then Satan could not possibly be there because it is "church." I beg to differ; he is at church, trying to keep anybody from coming forward to find victory. Satan is in the church, and unfortunately, he is also in many pulpits.

I have heard a story where there is a guy who comes into town and sees a big, fancy house sitting up on a hill. At the bottom of the hill, there is a demon sitting on the mailbox. As he comes further into town, he sees a rundown shack with three hundred demons as mad as they could be, up on the roof. The guy goes back to the demon sitting on the mailbox and says, "What is going on?"

The demon says, "These people up here are playing church, and we're just keeping an eye on them. Now at that shack in town, those people are down on their knees praying, and we're doing everything we can to try and stop them, but we're not having much luck."

This story can open our eyes to the fact that if Satan has you, then he's going to keep an eye on you; however, if he does not have you, then he is going to bring all the forces of hell against you. The Bible says that the gates of hell will not prevail against God's church. We do not enter the spiritual realm without fear and trembling unless we are prepared. Christians cannot have demons dwell in them because the Holy Spirit dwells in them.

Acts 28:1–9 says:

And when they were escaped, then they knew that the island was called Melita. And the barbarous people showed us no little kindness: for they kindeled a fire, and received us every one, because of the present rain, and because of the cold. And when Paul had gathered a bundle of sticks and laid them on the fire, there came a viper out of the heat, and fastened on his hand And when the barbarians saw the venomous beast hang on his hand, they said among themselves, No doubt this man is a murderer, whom, though he hath escaped the sea, yet vengeance suffereth not to live. And he shook off the beast into the fire, and felt no harm. Howbeit they looked when he should have swollen, or fallen down dead suddenly: but after they had looked a great while, and saw no harm come to him, they changed their minds, and said that he was a god. In the same quarters were possessions of the chief man of the island, whose name was Pub'li-us; who received us, and lodged us three days courteously. And it came to pass, that the father of Pub'li-us lay sick of a fever and of a bloody flux: to whom Paul entered in, and prayed, and laid his hands on him, and healed him. So when this was done, others also, which had diseases in the island, came, and were healed.

Acts 28:1–9 says that they were shipwrecked and were laying wood out on the fire when a viper struck Paul's hand. This caused them to think that he was an evil man; however, when Paul did not die, they then thought that he was a god. The scripture says that you shall take up serpents and they shall not hurt you. Does this mean that we all go out and handle serpents? No way. It was referring to the above illustration where if a serpent were to strike you, then God would protect you.

This reminds me of an incident that happened in my life some years ago. We were planning a fun-filled family afternoon at the lake, and when we got there, some men were cutting logs to clear the land. These logs were just the prefect size to fit in the trunk of the car. I decided to get some of these logs so that I would not have to buy firewood. First we were going to load up the trunk with logs, and then we would go play golf. When we went to load the wood, a poisonous spider bit me. My hand began to immediately swell up massively with red streaks shooting straight up. I had a vicious reaction to this bite. Then the scripture came to me; *"You shall take up serpents and they shall not hurt you."* I held out my hand and said, "In the name of Jesus, I rebuke this thing." I let my hand down, and the swelling and redness all disappeared.

John 14:7–12 says:

> If ye had known me, ye should have known my Father also: and from henceforth ye know him, and have seen him. Philip saith unto him, Lord, show us the Father, and it sufficeth us. Jesus saith unto him, Have I been so long time with you, and yet hast thou not known me, Philip? he that hath seen me hath seen the Father; and how sayest thou then, Show us the Father? Believest thou not that I am in the Father, and the Father in me? the words that I speak unto you I speak not of myself: but the Father that dwelleth in me, he doeth the works. Believe me that I am in the Father, and the Father in me: or else believe me for the very works' sake. Verily, verily, I say unto you, He that believeth on me, the works that I do shall he do also; and greater works than these shall he do; because I go unto my Father.

Sometimes I wonder how many of us at times do not know the Father because we do not know Jesus. Phillip walked with Jesus and still did not see the Father. The number one problem that Jesus had with his disciples is the number one problem that he has with you and me—he could not get them to get out of the flesh and into the Spirit. They wanted Jesus to come as the ruler and the king. They wanted him to set up a kingdom in which they could be a part of it. They could not see that he was establishing the spiritual kingdom that they needed.

How many times does God speak to us, and we do not hear? How many times does he show us something, and we do not see? We cannot see nor hear him because we are searching for the physical and not the spiritual. If we look up the definition of "the Word," we will see that it means a thought or concept, the expression or utterance of that thought. Therefore, to put it into context, Jesus Christ is the "expression" or "utterance" of God.

To see Christ is to see God. God revealed himself to us by sending his Son in the flesh, and the Word became flesh. To take this a step further, the Word anointed with the Holy Spirit becomes the living Christ. Jesus said, "He who eats of my flesh and drinks of my blood shall have everlasting life."

What did He mean by this? He meant that you must feed on my "Word" daily. To drink blood is to receive the forgiveness of sin. So then why do we search for the physical and not the spiritual? Because the flesh hungers for the flesh, and to seek victory over the flesh, we must put the flesh into subjection to the Spirit.

The Lord gave me an illustration of this, which starts by saying that before you get saved, everything you do is in the flesh. When you were born, if you were hungry or dirty or wanted anything, you cried, and it worked because someone responded. This taught us that the way to get results was to make noise; the squeaky wheel gets the grease. The problem is that some people go on this way for years and years and years. Then, with salvation, you have a spiritual birth. Finally, with death, the flesh dies, and you become a totally spiritual being. What happens in the meantime between salvation and death? We must work continuously to walk in victory over the flesh by yielding to the Spirit.

Isaiah 58:1–4 says:

> Cry aloud, spare not, lift up thy voice like a trumpet, and show my people their transgression, and the house of Jacob their sins. Yet they seek me daily, and delight to know my ways, as a nation that did righteousness, and forsook not the ordinance of their God: they ask of me the ordinances of justice; they take delight in approaching to God. Wherefore have we fasted, say they, and thou seest not? wherefore have we afflicted our soul, and thou takest no knowledge? Behold, in the day of your fast ye find pleasure, and exact all your labors. Behold, ye fast for strife and debate, and to smite with the fist of wickedness: ye shall not fast as ye do this day, to make your voice to be heard on high.

Back when I first got saved, fasting was a very "in" thing to do. All my friends were doing it. There were even people who were writing books, telling of how they fasted for forty days and forty nights. These books were saying that unless you did this, you would never receive the power from God. Their basis for saying this was that Jesus did it and Moses did it too. What I discovered about most of the people who were fasting was that they were fasting because they needed an answer from God. They thought that they had to fast to get an answer from him. I do not serve that kind of God. He knows my thoughts and needs even before I ask him.

Luke 11:11–13 says:

> If a son shall ask bread of any of you that is a father, will he give him a stone? Or if he ask a fish, will he for a fish give him a serpent. Or if he shall ask an egg, will he offer him a scorpion? If ye then, being evil, know how to give good gifts unto your children: how much more shall your heavenly Father give the Holy Spirit to them that ask him?

My heavenly Father knows me, hears me, and will answer me because he loves me. I do not have to fast to get an answer from God. There is so much misconception today which allows people to get caught up in something that is an experience instead of what the scripture says. Many false doctrines today are built on experiences and not on God's Word. Some people take an experience and make a doctrine out of it because they can find scriptures to support it. This is Satan leading them astray. If you yield yourself to Satan, Satan will manifest himself. I hate to see people tormented and destroyed because somebody took an experience and built a doctrine out of it. I would advise you to search the scriptures to find out if what I am teaching you is true; and if I am wrong, then please come to me and let me know. I can be and have been wrong.

The point that I am trying to make is that this man was saying, "I am going to starve myself until God hears me." Our God does not work like this. We do not have to starve ourselves for him to hear us.

Isaiah 58:5–11 says:

Is it such a fast that I have chosen? a day for a man to afflict his soul? is it to bow down his head as a bulrush, and to spread sackcloth and ashes under him? wilt thou call this a fast, and an acceptable day to the Lord? Is not this the fast that I have chosen? to loose the bands of wickedness, to undo the heavy burdens, and to let the oppressed go free, and that ye break every yoke? Is it not to deal thy bread to the hungry, and that thou bring the poor that are cast out to thy house? when thou seest the naked, that thou cover him; and that thou hide not thyself from thine own flesh? Then shall thy light break forth as the morning, and thine health shall spring forth speedily: and thy righteousness shall go before thee; the glory of the Lord shall be thy rearward. Then shalt thou call, and the Lord shall answer; thou shalt cry, and he shall say, Here I am. If thou take away from the midst of thee the yoke, the putting forth of the finger, and speaking vanity; and if thou draw out thy soul to the hungry, and satisfy the afflicted soul; then shall thy light rise in obscurity, and thy darkness be as the noonday: and the Lord shall guide thee continually, and satisfy thy soul in drought, and make fat thy bones: and thou shalt be like a watered garden, and like a spring of water, whose waters fail not.

In Second Chronicles 7:14, God says that if his people, which means you and I, would humble themselves, and turn from their wicked ways, then he would hear from heaven. You may say, "But, I'm not wicked." What about unbelief? We are filled with unbelief which breaks God's heart much more than telling a lie. Why? Simply because we are so caught up in the world and desensitized due to the things that are happening that we have lost sight of our first love and of God. We've got to get on our knees, get into his Word, and find the things that God wants us to do. Then we can walk with him and have the strength and the power that he wants us to have.

To do this will take a total commitment. I used to say that when you got saved, it did not cost you anything, but it does; it costs you your life. When a person is truly drawn by the Holy Spirit, you could hold a gun to their head and tell them that if they pray to the Holy Spirit, you'll shoot them, and they would say, "Shoot me." One of the problems affecting salvation today is that we try to make it enticing, so we water it down instead of obeying God's unchanging Word. There are a lot of people who have come to Christ before they are ready. Be certain that you are ready and then make the commitment.

Isaiah 58:12–14 says:

> And they that shall be of thee shall build the old waste places: thou shalt raise up the foundations of many generations; and thou shalt be called, The repairer of the breach, The restorer of paths to dwell in. If thou turn away thy foot from the sabbath, from doing thy pleasure on my holy day; and call the sabbath a delight, the holy of the Lord, honorable; and shalt honor him, not doing thine own ways, nor finding thine own pleasure, nor speaking thine own words: then shalt thou delight thyself in the Lord; and I will cause thee to ride upon the high places of the earth, and feed thee with the heritage of Jacob thy father: for the mouth of the Lord hath spoken it.

If only we could follow the passage above which says, "Delight ourselves in the Lord."

Hebrews 2:4 says:

> God also bearing them witness, both with signs and wonders, and with divers miracles, and gifts of the Holy Ghost, according to his own will?

This is exactly how God does it. He does it according to his own will. As we look back on the disciples, we see that they sold everything that they had so that the only thing left was a total commitment to God. For two to three years, I fought with this scripture. I almost lost my practice because I was so "sold out" to the Lord that I was not tending to my practice.

If it were not for God's grace, we would have starved to death. I got saved and filled with the Holy Spirit, and the next thing I knew was that I wanted to go to Russia to smuggle in Bibles. I wanted to do all these things and be on the front line of action. I had no fear, but I did have a family and a responsibility. At least I had enough sense to realize that I did have a responsibility to take care of my family. I struggled and struggled because I had friends going overseas to missions and various exciting places. Then, one day, I went into the dark room to develop an X-ray. While there, God spoke to me, saying, "All of your friends are going overseas and doing exciting things, but who will stay here?"

I said to God, "I will, I will stay here."

Then He said to me, "You stay here, and I will let you see exciting things. Just be faithful."

So I did stay, but I wondered how in today's world I could give universally and still make a living. Then I realized that God puts us in the place where we are. In my world today, as a businessman, I am given the opportunity to witness to many people every day. I know that I am successful, so there must be something to it. Is not this some of the confirmation that God says? It is the same in all our lives; we all have the same witness.

At times, we may feel that God is not using us, but do not be so sure; somebody is watching us. Whether we know it or not, each of us influences somebody's life by just living daily for Jesus Christ. I think that God wants us to take it a step further and say, "Okay, God, I want to make that commitment."

# CURSE AND REBELLION

After I came to understand that there are seven types of illnesses in the Scriptures, God then allowed me to pray the prayer of faith and do so with the mind of Christ. In this book, we are going to explore the seven illnesses described in the Bible. The first illness described in the scriptures came into existence because of sin. I have labeled it "Curse and Rebellion."

Genesis 3:1–3 says:

> Now the serpent was more subtile than any beast of the field which the Lord God had made. And he said unto the woman, Yea, hath God said, Ye shall not eat of every tree of the garden? And the woman said unto the serpent, We may eat of the fruit of the trees of the garden: but of the fruit of the tree which is in the midst of the garden, God hath said, Ye shall not eat of it, neither shall ye touch it, lest ye die.

If you will notice in the passage above, the woman said that you shall not eat of it nor "touch" it or you shall die; God never said anything about "touching" the forbidden tree. Once again, I would like to reflect on the book of Revelation.

Revelation 22:18 says:

> For I testify unto every man that heareth the words of the prophecy of this book, If any man shall add unto these things, God shall add unto him the plagues that are written in this book.

I find it remarkably interesting how you can read the first passage in the first book of the Bible, and then read the last passage in the last book of the Bible to see the very same message. When I look at Eve and other people who are mentioned in the Old Testament, I try to find "good things" to identify with, but I always seem to identify more with their shortcomings. This, for me, is very typical and shows that sometimes we do not have enough faith in ourselves. Just as God said to Eve that you are not to eat of it, and then she added that she must also not "touch" it.

Genesis 3:4–5 says:

> And the serpent said unto the woman, Ye shall not surely die: for God doth know that in the day ye eat thereof, then your eyes shall be opened, and ye shall be as gods, knowing good and evil.

Satan, in the form of a serpent, said to Eve that she will not die physically if she eats of the forbidden tree. He knows that she will die spiritually.

Genesis 3:6-13 says:

> And when the woman saw that the tree was good for food, and that it was pleasant to the eyes, and a tree to be desired to make one wise, she took of the fruit thereof, and did eat, and gave also unto her husband with her; and he did eat. And the eyes of them both were opened, and they knew that they were naked; and they sewed fig leaves together, and made themselves aprons. And they heard the voice of the Lord God walking in the garden in the cool of the day: and Adam and his wife hid themselves from the presence of the Lord God amongst the trees of the garden. And the Lord God called unto Adam, and said unto him, Where art thou? And he said, I heard thy voice in the garden, and I was afraid, because I was naked; and I hid myself. And he said, Who told thee that thou wast naked? Hast thou eaten of the tree, whereof I commanded thee that thou shouldest not eat? And the man said, The woman whom thou gavest to be with me,

she gave me of the tree, and I did eat. And the Lord God said unto the woman, What is this that thou hast done? And the woman said, The serpent beguiled me, and I did eat.

In the passage above, we see man blame God for his disobedience. Adam literally said to God that he ate the forbidden fruit because of the woman whom God gave him; meaning that if God had not given him this woman who was so imperfect, then it would never have happened. This is man's first case of "passing the buck" instead of owning up to his mistake and saying, "God, I have sinned."

Additionally, we also see the woman blame God for her disobedience by saying to God that if he had not made the snake, then she would not have sinned. This is a classic example of how we blame God when we make a wrong choice.

One time, as I was really struggling, God said to me, "You keep on sinning because you love your sins. If you didn't love it, then you wouldn't keep doing it." This was a rude awakening for me, realizing that I loved to sin. I loved to sin because it was easier to sin and because I did not fear God. Sometimes we convince ourselves that God is not going to judge our sin and that we can "get by" with it. This puts us in a grave situation. The fear of the Lord is the hatred of sin. In other words, if you do not hate sin, then you do not fear God; and if we do not fear God, then we keep on sinning.

The result of sin is death. When we can finally come to the point of hating anything that separates us from the fullness, love, joy, and peace of God, then there is victory. What we must do is develop such an intimate relationship with God that we detest anything that separates us from it. Then it's easier to walk in God's righteousness than it was when we were trying to live partly in sin.

Genesis 3:14–21 says:

And the Lord God said unto the serpent, Because thou hast done this, thou art cursed above all cattle, and above every beast of the field; upon thy belly shalt thou go, and dust shalt thou eat all the days of thy life: and I will put enmity between thee and the woman, and between thy seed and her seed; it shall bruise thy head, and thou shalt bruise his heel. Unto the woman he said, I will greatly multiply thy sorrow and thy conception; in sorrow thou shalt bring forth children; and thy desire shall be to thy husband, and he shall rule over thee. And unto Adam he said, Because thou hast hearkened unto the voice of thy wife, and hast eaten of the tree, of which I commanded thee, saying, Thou shalt not eat of it: cursed is the ground for thy sake; in sorrow shalt thou eat of it all the days of thy life; thorns also and thistles shall it bring forth to thee; and thou shalt eat the herb of the field: in the sweat of thy face shalt thou eat bread, till thou return unto the ground; for out of it wast thou taken: for dust thou art, and unto dust shalt thou return. And Adam called his wife's name Eve; because she was the mother of all living. Unto Adam also and to his wife did the Lord God make coats of skins, and clothed them.

I would like for us to understand the non-spiritual because, as the book of Corinthians says, we can understand the non-spiritual because we were once non-spiritual. In other words, we have been there; but our problem is that we forget we have been there. For example, if a situation arises where a child dies, then we might say, "Why? They are innocent. Why do they have to suffer?"

If we do not have Christ in our lives, then we may never get over it. If we put ourselves in the life of someone who does not know Christ, then we can understand their hurt, anger, and what they are going through. Then ask God to give us love and compassion so that we can reach them where they are at.

The point that I am trying to make is that sometimes we may just "go through the motions" of knowing God. But when a crisis comes, we first get angry with God. Then we get on our knees and find a relationship with him. When this finally happens, God begins to mold us into his image. Christ learned obedience through suffering. So if the Son of God learned it through suffering, then there is not much hope for us to learn it any other way. If you have ever prayed to God, saying that you would like to be "just like Jesus," then you have opened the door for God to mold you into his image. "What does this mean?" you might ask. It means that he is going to get us to forget trusting in our own thoughts, our own strengths, our own power, our own knowledge, and start trusting him.

There has been once or twice in my life when I could not pray anymore; I did not have any faith left. The only thing I could do was say to God, "You're in control, and I surrender." The one thing I knew was that if God was in control, and I died, then I would be with him. Unfortunately, what happens is that when we finally get to the point of giving God total control of our lives, we look around and take a handful back. We just cannot seem to leave it at the altar. If we could just totally surrender and leave it at the cross, then we could make it.

Genesis 3:22–24 says:

> And the Lord God said, Behold, the man is become as one of us, to know good and evil: and now, lest he put forth his hand, and take also of the tree of life and eat, and live for ever: therefore the Lord God sent him forth from the garden of Eden, to till the ground from whence he was taken. So he drove out the man: and he placed at the east of the garden of Eden cherubim, and a flaming sword which turned every way, to keep the way of the tree of life.

A common misconception about this scripture is that God cast Adam and Eve out of the garden because of their sin. God did not cast Adam and Eve out of the garden because of sin, but he did it to save man from living forever in sin. Adam and Eve had the knowledge of the tree of life, and to protect man from living in his sin forever, God had to cast them out. Thank goodness he did because otherwise we would have been condemned to living in this world for eternity.

Sin entered the world when Adam and Eve ate the fruit of the tree of knowledge of good and evil. This resulted in pain with childbirth. In Genesis 1 and 2, God said that everything was good, and he blessed Adam and Eve. The world went from a blessing to a curse when man sinned. With the original sin, as it is often referred to, man now would die and not live forever. The aging process began at this time and along with it many diseases. Up until this time, there was no disease, and man was not to die. We find in the book of Genesis instances where men have lived to be well over nine hundred years of age; however, as man continued to live in sin, we see that age began to decline. Finally we see that God drastically declined man's age.

Psalm 90:10 says:

> The days of our lives *are* seventy years; And if by reason of strength *they are* eighty years, Yet their boast *is* only labor and sorrow; For it is soon cut off, and we fly away.

I would like for us also to look at what rebellion does because this comes in as part of the original sin.

First Samuel 5:1–6 says:

> And the Philistines took the ark of God, and brought it from Ebene'zer unto Ashdod. When the Philistines took the ark of God, they brought it into the house of Dagon, and set it by Dagon. And when they of Ashdod arose early on the morrow, behold, Dagon was fallen upon his face to the earth before the ark of the Lord. And they took Dagon, and set him in his place again. And when they arose early on the morrow morning, behold, Dagon was fallen upon his face to the ground before the ark of the Lord; and the head of Dagon and both the palms of his hands were cut off upon the threshold; only the stump of Dagon was left to him. Therefore neither the priests of Dagon, nor any that come into Dagon's house, tread on the threshold of Dagon in Ashdod unto this day. But the hand of the Lord was heavy upon them of Ashdod, and he destroyed them, and smote them with emerods, even Ashdod and the coasts thereof.

We see that when the ark of God was captured and put amongst the idols of Ashdod that God kept knocking down their god. Finally, when they would not recognize that there is a superior God, he struck them with hemorrhoids.

First Samuel 5:7–12 says:

> And when the men of Ashdod saw that it was so, they said, The ark of the God of Israel shall not abide with us: for

his hand is sore upon us, and upon Dagon our god. They sent therefore and gathered all the lords of the Philistines unto them, and said, What shall we do with the ark of the God of Israel? And they answered, Let the ark of the God of Israel be carried about unto Gath. And they carried the ark of the God of Israel about thither. And it was so, that, after they had carried it about, the hand of the Lord was against the city with a very great destruction: and he smote the men of the city, both small and great, and they had emerods in their secret parts. Therefore they sent the ark of God to Ekron. And it came to pass, as the ark of God came to Ekron, that the Ek'ronites cried out, saying, They have brought about the ark of the God of Israel to us, to slay us and our people. So they sent and gathered together all the lords of the Philistines, and said, Send away the ark of the God of Israel, and let it go again to his own place, that it slay us not, and our people: for there was a deadly destruction throughout all the city; the hand of God was very heavy there. And the men that died not were smitten with the emerods: and the cry of the city went up to heaven.

Notice what happens here. In the beginning, they would not recognize the superiority of God, and so God brought judgment. Then, finally, they recognized the hand of God and concluded that they had better get rid of the ark from their presence or be doomed to die. In short, their rebellion against God resulted in hemorrhoids and death because they defied God. This shows us that it is a serious thing to defy him.

Exodus 15:26 says:

And said, If thou wilt diligently hearken to the voice of the Lord thy God, and wilt do that which is right in his sight, and wilt give ear to his commandments, and keep all his statutes, I will put none of these diseases upon thee, which I have brought upon the Egyptians: for I am the Lord that healeth thee.

The Egyptians served idols, and God brought many diseases upon them because of it. God warns the Israelites that if they rebel against his commandments, they will have the same diseases.

Deuteronomy 28:15–29 says:

> But it shall come to pass, if thou wilt not hearken unto the voice of the Lord thy God, to observe to do all his commandments and his statutes which I command thee this day; that all these curses shall come upon thee, and overtake thee: Cursed shalt thou be in the city, and cursed shalt thou be in the field. Cursed shall be thy basket and thy store. Cursed shall be the fruit of thy body, and the fruit of thy land, the increase of thy kine, and the flocks of thy sheep. Cursed shalt thou be when thou comest in, and cursed shalt thou be when thou goest out. The Lord shall send upon thee cursing, vexation, and rebuke, in all that thou settest thine hand unto for to do, until thou be destroyed, and until thou perish quickly; because of the wickedness of thy doings, whereby thou hast forsaken me. The Lord shall make the pestilence cleave unto thee, until he have consumed thee from off the land, whither thou goest to possess it. The Lord shall smite thee with a consumption, and with a fever, and with an inflammation, and with an extreme burning, and with the sword, and with blasting, and with mildew; and they shall pursue thee until thou perish. And thy heaven that is over thy head shall be brass, and the earth that is under thee shall be iron. The Lord shall make the rain of thy land powder and dust: from heaven shall it come down upon thee, until thou be destroyed. The Lord shall cause thee to be smitten before thine enemies: thou shalt go out one way against them, and flee seven ways before them: and shalt be removed into all the kingdoms of the earth. And thy carcase shall be meat unto all fowls of the air, and unto the beasts of the earth, and no man shall fray them away. The Lord will smite thee with the botch of Egypt, and with the emerods, and with the scab, and with the itch, whereof thou canst not be healed. The Lord shall

smite thee with madness, and blindness, and astonishment of heart: And thou shalt grope at noonday, as the blind gropeth in darkness, and thou shalt not prosper in thy ways: and thou shalt be only oppressed and spoiled evermore, and no man shall save thee.

In the passages above, God is saying to the nation of Israel that if they do not obey him, then they will be cursed. As we know, Israel did not obey God. So the curse came upon them and with it all the diseases, afflictions, and problems that they had been warned of by God. With the original sin, man lost his communion with God. Prior to original sin, man walked with God daily. After original sin, man hid from God. When man does not communicate with God, he becomes self-centered and walks in his own righteousness. With self- righteousness comes rebellion and the curse.

Deuteronomy 11:26–28 says:

> Behold, I set before you this day a blessing and a curse; a blessing, if ye obey the commandments of the Lord your God, which I command you this day: and a curse, if ye will not obey the commandments of the Lord your God, but turn aside out of the way which I command you this day, to go after other gods, which ye have not known.

In this passage, God lays it right out. He says that there will be a blessing if you obey him and a curse if you go after other gods or idols.

Jeremiah 44:21–23 says:

> The incense that ye burned in the cities of Judah, and in the streets of Jerusalem, ye and your fathers, your kings and your princes, and the people of the land, did not the Lord remember them, and came it not into his mind? so that the Lord could no longer bear, because of the evil of your doings, and because of the abominations which ye have committed; therefore is your land a desolation, and an astonishment, and a curse, without an inhabitant, as at this day. Because ye have burned incense, and because ye have sinned against the Lord, and have not obeyed the voice of the Lord, nor walked in his

law, nor in his statutes, nor in his testimonies; therefore this evil is happened unto you, as at this day.

I know that a lot of people would like for us to believe today that after you accept Jesus Christ as your Lord and Savior that there will be no more judgment. In other words, you would be free to do whatever you want to do. But what about the scripture that says you sin willfully after you come to know Christ?

Hebrews 10:26 says:

> For if we sin willfully after we have received the knowledge of the truth, there no longer remains a sacrifice for sins.

I know that there are things in my life that have happened to me because I was not obedient to the Lord. God made it truly clear to me. I had some things in my life that were not right, and God was dealing with me. I was ignoring him, and finally, I developed asthma so badly that I could hardly even exist. All the medicine I could take would not make it any better. I finally repented, turning to the Lord and saying, "God, you've got my attention."

The Lord then said to me, "For seven days you are going to suffer like you have never suffered before, and then I will relieve you." And he did just that. Although God may choose to heal us, there may still be consequences for our sin. Miriam and Aaron spoke against Moses. God made Miriam leprous for seven days before restoring her.

Numbers 12:1–2 says:

> Then Miriam and Aaron spoke against Moses because of the Ethiopian woman whom he had married; for he had married an Ethiopian woman. So they said, "Has the Lord indeed spoken only through Moses? Has He not spoken through us also?" And the Lord heard *it.*

Numbers 12:9–14 says:

> So the anger of the Lord was aroused against them, and He departed. And when the cloud departed from above the tabernacle, suddenly Miriam *became* leprous, as *white as* snow.

Then Aaron turned toward Miriam, and there she was, a leper. So Aaron said to Moses, "Oh, my lord! Please do not lay *this* sin on us, in which we have done foolishly and in which we have sinned. "Please do not let her be as one dead, whose flesh is half consumed when he comes out of his mother's womb!" So Moses cried out to the Lord, saying, "Please heal her, O God, I pray!" Then the Lord said to Moses, "If her father had but spit in her face, would she not be shamed seven days? Let her be shut out of the camp seven days, and afterward she may be received *again.*"

It is so easy today for us to just go to the doctor. Do not misunderstand what I am saying. I mean that if you are sick, then go to the doctor; but you must pray about it too. It is no mystery when we sin; we know when we are not right with God. I have seen people at the altar saying, "Oh God, show me my sin." What we should be saying is, "God, I know my sin, but help me to wake up. Show me what to do about it." We must also be very careful when we are praying for someone else because they could be in a total state of rebellion, and unless we have discernment, we may be praying for something that could actually be inhibiting the work of God.

There was a lady who was as thin as a rail in a church that I was once attending. She was just skin and bone and was sick all the time. Every time the altar was open, she was there. An evangelist came in one day and conducted a healing service in which she joined the prayer line. When he got to her, he just completely stopped and did not move. He said to her, "Ma'am, when you will forgive your ex-husband, God will heal you."

She fell on her face. He did not let compassion get in the way. He just delivered God's message as straight as he received it. This is an example of how we must walk with the boldness and communication with God so that we can hear from him which not will only help ourselves but help our brothers and sisters too.

Daniel 9:9–11 says:

To the Lord our God belong mercies and forgivenesses, though we have rebelled against him; neither have we obeyed the voice of the Lord our God, to walk in his laws, which he set before us by his servants the prophets. Yea, all Israel have transgressed thy law, even by departing, that they might not obey thy voice; therefore the curse is poured upon us, and the oath that is written in the law of Moses the servant of God, because we have sinned against him.

Above is Daniel's recording of what Moses said happened to Israel. Malachi 2:2 says:

If ye will not hear, and if ye will not lay it to heart, to give glory unto my name, saith the Lord of hosts, I will even send a curse upon you, and I will curse your blessings: yea, I have cursed them already, because ye do not lay it to heart.

In the passage above, he is saying that if you do not give him the glory and you do not hear, not only will he curse you, but he will also curse your blessings and has already done it.

Malachi 3:9 says:

Ye are cursed with a curse: for ye have robbed me, even this whole nation.

Exodus 20:1–6 says:

And God spake all these words, saying, I am the Lord thy God, which have brought thee out of the land of Egypt, out of the house of bondage. Thou shalt have no other gods before me. Thou shalt not make unto thee any graven image, or any likeness of any thing that is in heaven above, or that is in the earth beneath, or that is in the water under the earth: thou shalt not bow down thyself to them, nor serve them: for I the Lord thy God am a jealous God, visiting the iniquity of the fathers upon the children unto the third and fourth generation of them that hate me; and showing mercy unto thousands of them that love me, and keep my commandments.

We must remember something that happened as Jesus walked upon the earth; the disciples were always pointing to someone and asking who sinned. Jesus says that this should not happen. We should not put judgment on others and should not overlook the reality that if we have idols, we open ourselves to the judgment of God. When a man's heart is turned away from God and his Word, man loses the blessing of God and is cursed.

God is a jealous God, visiting the sin of the fathers upon the third and fourth generations. For example, when a man becomes an alcoholic, he has committed idolatry. "Why?" you may ask. It is because he is looking for something to relax him, but God has promised that in his Son, Jesus Christ. Alcohol becomes an idol to him, and most likely, his son and grandson will become alcoholics too.

Today's society would like for us to call alcoholism a disease rather than calling sin a sin. Therefore we have become a society of excuse makers when we say that our sin is due to our inheritance, our environment, or that someone else made us do it. We see in the Scriptures that God's Word is clear in stating that if we sin, it may have effects on our family. It is of extreme importance that man comes to grip with his sin problem. A man's greatest struggle is trying to keep the law, and the harder he tries, the greater the failure. In short, man is in desperate need of a Savior.

A psychiatrist in the state of Texas said that half of the mental institutions could be emptied if preachers would preach on sin. Do not misunderstand this statement. He does not deny that mental illness is a real disease but points out that a lot of cases are merely sin and guilt that a person just cannot seem to get rid of.

I have a good friend who is a psychiatrist. To my knowledge, he does not know Jesus as his Christ and Savior, but he uses the Bible as the guideline for his psychiatric practice. It is amazing to watch this man work. I've heard him say, "Okay, so you have a problem. What's the worst thing that could happen to you?" He said, "I'm not interested in all of your past and why you came to this place. I want to know what you're going to do about it today." He said, "The past is water under the bridge, and there is nothing that you can do about it. But you have today, tomorrow, and the rest of your life. So, what are you going to do about it?"

Pretty strong counsel, isn't it? Isn't this true with us today? So what if someone wronged us yesterday? Are we going to live in the past and continue to blame? Or are we going to say, "Okay, God, I give it to you, and now you give me the power in Christ to live and forgive." I am sure that all of us have had things happen in our lives that could make us very, very bitter, as I have, but I chose not to let them. I realized that I was the only person who was going to get hurt and that the people who did it to me did not care. It is apparent that the only choice is to forgive and go on.

I had an experience several years ago when I was seeing a doctor. After seeing him for a while, I began to realize that he was doing me more harm than good. In addition to my seeing him, he was also bringing his dog to see me. The dog was suffering from congestive heart failure. I called his office one day after having a severe reaction to an overdose of a medication that he had given me. I said, "I need to speak with the doctor."

"Well, you can't speak with the doctor," the receptionist replied.

I then said, "I'm going to stay on the phone until I can talk to him because it is very important that I speak with him."

This went on and on and on. Finally he got on the phone and told me that I was absolutely the worst patient that he'd ever had and that there has never been anyone who even comes close to being as bad a patient as I was. I will admit that, at times, I am not the best patient; but in this situation, I was following his orders exactly. He went on to tell me that he thought I was absolutely the worst veterinarian that he had ever seen, that his dog didn't have congestive heart failure, that I was killing his dog, and that he took his dog off the medication that I had prescribed. He berated me for quite some time, and then I said to him, "Well, sir, I'm still asking for you to transfer my records."

Each time I asked him this, he would start in all over again. I was probably on the phone with him for an hour and a half, going through this same routine. Finally he said, "So you want your records transferred."

I said, "Yes, sir."

That night, I was at the animal hospital, treating an emergency when he called my house. He said that his dog had just had a heart attack and was dying. He asked my wife if I would see the dog. She told him that she really did not know if I would see him or not but that she would call me and find out. When she did, I told her that I would see his dog if he really, really wanted me to but that I was already working on another animal. If he would come to the hospital, I would see his dog when I finished.

He came to the hospital with his dog, and immediately, we tried to save the dog's life. Unfortunately, I could not, and the dog died of heart failure. He could not understand how I could forgive him, try to console him, and take care of his dog. He left the hospital, saying, "I just can't understand how you could be so nice to me after the way I treated you today." The moral to this story is that we must forgive.

Galatians 3:10–13 says:

> For as many as are of the works of the law are under the curse: for it is written, Cursed is every one that continueth not in all things which are written in the book of the law to do them. But that no man is justified by the law in the sight of God, it is evident: for, The just shall live by faith. And the law is not of faith: but, The man that doeth them shall live in them. Christ hath redeemed us from the curse of the law, being made a curse for us: for it is written, Cursed is every one that hangeth on a tree.

We learn in the passage above that to be redeemed from the curse of the law, we must live by faith as it is written in the Holy Bible.

Revelation 22:3 says:

> And there shall be no more curse: but the throne of God and of the Lamb shall be in it; and his servants shall serve him.

As we come to the end of time, God says that there will be no more curse. Praise be to God because the curse hung upon the tree. It was Christ who took our curse and paid our debt. When we accept Jesus as our Lord and Savior, the curse is broken, and God's blessing is upon us to the third and fourth generation. What a wonderful God we have. He said that the curse came for our own good and to bring us to Christ at which point he breaks that curse.

Isaiah 53:4–5 says:

> Surely he hath borne our griefs, and carried our sorrows:
> yet we did esteem him stricken, smitten of God, and afflicted.
> But he was wounded for our transgressions, he was bruised
> for our iniquities: the chastisement of our peace was upon
> him; and with his stripes we are healed.

What we find as we go through this scripture is that for everything
that God brought about, He also brought about the change. For
example, when man sinned, the curse came; when Christ came, the
curse was broken, and the door was opened so that we no longer had to
live under the curse. When Jesus went to the cross, he died for all our
sins, including the original sin, and by his stripes we are healed.

Romans 5:12–21 says:

> Wherefore, as by one man sin entered into the world,
> and death by sin; and so death passed upon all men, for that
> all have sinned: (For until the law sin was in the world: but
> sin is not imputed when there is no law. Nevertheless death
> reigned from Adam to Moses, even over them that had not
> sinned after the similitude of Adam's transgression, who is
> the figure of him that was to come. But not as the offence, so
> also is the free gift. For if through the offence of one many
> be dead, much more the grace of God, and the gift by grace,
> which is by one man, Jesus Christ, hath abounded unto
> many. And not as it was by one that sinned, so is the gift:
> for the judgment was by one to condemnation, but the free
> gift is of many offences unto justification. For if by one man's
> offence death reigned by one; much more they which receive
> abundance of grace and of the gift of righteousness shall reign
> in life by one, Jesus Christ.) Therefore as by the offence of
> one judgment came upon all men to condemnation; even so
> by the righteousness of one the free gift came upon all men
> unto justification of life. For as by one man's disobedience
> many were made sinners, so by the obedience of one shall
> many be made righteous. Moreover the law entered, that the

offence might abound. But where sin abounded, grace did much more abound: That as sin hath reigned unto death, even so might grace reign through righteousness unto eternal life by Jesus Christ our Lord.

I do not know whether anybody else has ever done this, but I used to, at times, become angry with Adam because of his sin. I thought that if Adam and Eve had not sinned, then we would not be in this predicament. Now I say to myself, "Oh yes, we would have because if they hadn't sinned, then I would have." When we all come to realize that we have all sinned and come short of the glory of God, then we understand this. We also learn in this passage that when sin entered in, it brought death; and when Christ came, he brought life. We can thank God that by the grace of God, when we accept Jesus Christ as our Lord and Savior, we put on his righteousness.

# ILLNESS UNTO DEATH

The second illness described in the Scriptures is the illness unto death. Let us now explore this topic through the following passages.

Ecclesiastes 3:1–2 says:

> To every thing there is a season, and a time to every purpose under the heaven: A time to be born, and a time to die; a time to plant, and a time to pluck up that which is planted.

God has a time for everything. The hardest thing for us to face is death. To be honest, the only time we want to die is when everything is going wrong. "Lord, get me out of this mess." For the Christian, death ushers us into our reward. Because we have such a strong survival mode, we pray for healing and do not want to consider that God may be calling us home to be with him. Paul says that he would rather be with God but that God left him here to be a benefit to the Christians. Thank goodness for this fact; we now have a large portion of the Bible because God did not call him home right away.

Second Samuel 12:1–23 says:

> And the Lord sent Nathan unto David. And he came unto him, and said unto him, There were two men in one city; the one rich, and the other poor. The rich man had exceeding many flocks and herds: But the poor man had nothing, save one little ewe lamb, which he had bought and nourished up: and it grew up together with him, and with

his children; it did eat of his own meat, and drank of his own cup, and lay in his bosom, and was unto him as a daughter. And there came a traveller unto the rich man, and he spared to take of his own flock and of his own herd, to dress for the wayfaring man that was come unto him; but took the poor man's lamb, and dressed it for the man that was come to him. And David's anger was greatly kindled against the man; and he said to Nathan, As the Lord liveth, the man that hath done this thing shall surely die: And he shall restore the lamb fourfold, because he did this thing, and because he had no pity. And Nathan said to David, Thou art the man. Thus saith the Lord God of Israel, I anointed thee king over Israel, and I delivered thee out of the hand of Saul; And I gave thee thy master's house, and thy master's wives into thy bosom, and gave thee the house of Israel and of Judah; and if that had been too little, I would moreover have given unto thee such and such things. Wherefore hast thou despised the commandment of the Lord, to do evil in his sight? thou hast killed Uriah the Hittite with the sword, and hast taken his wife to be thy wife, and hast slain him with the sword of the children of Ammon. Now therefore the sword shall never depart from thine house; because thou hast despised me, and hast taken the wife of Uriah the Hittite to be thy wife. Thus saith the Lord, Behold, I will raise up evil against thee out of thine own house, and I will take thy wives before thine eyes, and give them unto thy neighbour, and he shall lie with thy wives in the sight of this sun. For thou didst it secretly: but I will do this thing before all Israel, and before the sun. And David said unto Nathan, I have sinned against the Lord. And Nathan said unto David, The Lord also hath put away thy sin; thou shalt not die. Howbeit, because by this deed thou hast given great occasion to the enemies of the Lord to blaspheme, the child also that is born unto thee shall surely die. And Nathan departed unto his house. And the Lord struck the child that Uriah's wife bare unto David, and it was very sick. David therefore besought God for the child; and David fasted, and went in, and lay all night upon the earth. And the elders of his house arose, and went to him, to raise him up from the earth: but he would not, neither did he eat bread with them. And it came to pass on the seventh day, that the child died. And the servants of David feared to tell him that the child was dead: for they said, Behold, while the child was yet alive, we spake unto him, and he would not hearken unto our voice: how will he then vex himself, if we tell him that the child is dead? But when David saw that his servants whispered, David perceived that the child was dead: therefore David said unto his servants, Is the child dead? And they said, He is dead. Then David arose from the earth, and washed, and anointed himself, and changed his apparel, and came into the house of the Lord, and worshipped: then he came to his own house; and when he required, they set bread before him, and he did eat. Then said his servants unto him, What thing is this that thou hast done? thou didst fast and weep for the child, while it was alive; but when the child was dead, thou didst rise and eat bread. And he said, While the child was yet alive, I fasted and wept: for I said, Who can tell whether GOD will be gracious to me, that the child may live? But now he is dead, wherefore should I fast? can I bring him back again? I shall go to him, but he shall not return to me.

God told David, through Nathan the prophet, that his child would die. David decided to intercede anyway. He fasted and prayed for seven days, praying that God would change his mind. God said to David that his child had the illness unto death, and his child died. Notice that after his child died, David went into the house of the Lord and worshipped. Also notice that David said the child could not come to him but that he could go to the child, meaning that in the end, he would be where the child was.

Second Kings 20:1–3 says:

In those days was Hezekiah sick unto death. And the prophet Isaiah the son of Amoz came to him, and said unto him, Thus saith the Lord, Set thine house in order; for thou shalt die, and not live. Then he turned his face to the wall, and prayed unto the Lord, saying, I beseech thee, O Lord, remember now how I have walked before thee in truth and with a perfect heart, and have done that which is good in thy sight. And Hezekiah wept sore.

I would like for us to notice something here because I feel that it is especially important as we explore this scripture. Hezekiah turns to God and says, "Look at all I have done for you." Through the testimony and scriptures that we have studied thus far, we have learned that God is not really impressed with what we have done for him. Sometimes we need to be careful when we think that we have done great things for God. As we go further, I am sure that you will begin to see what I mean by this.

Second Kings 20:4–21 says:

And it came to pass, afore Isaiah was gone out into the middle court, that the word of the Lord came to him, saying, Turn again, and tell Hezekiah the captain of my people, Thus saith the Lord, the God of David thy father, I have heard thy prayer, I have seen thy tears: behold, I will heal thee: on the third day thou shalt go up unto the house of the Lord. And I will add unto thy days fifteen years; and I will deliver thee and this city out of the hand of the king of Assyria; and I will defend this city for mine own sake, and for my servant David's sake. And Isaiah said, Take a lump of figs. And they took and laid it on the boil, and he recovered. And Hezekiah said unto Isaiah, What shall be the sign that the Lord will heal me, and that I shall go up into the house of the Lord the third day? And Isaiah said, This sign shalt thou have of the Lord, that the Lord will do the thing that he hath spoken: shall the shadow go forward ten degrees, or go back ten degrees? And Hezekiah answered, It is a light thing for the shadow to go down ten degrees: nay, but let the shadow return backward ten degrees. And Isaiah the prophet cried unto the Lord: and he brought the shadow ten degrees backward, by which it had gone down in the dial of Ahaz. At that time Berodachbaladan, the son of Baladan, king of Babylon, sent letters and a present unto Hezekiah: for he had heard that Hezekiah had been sick. And Hezekiah hearkened unto them, and shewed them all the house of his precious things, the silver, and the gold, and the spices, and the precious ointment, and all the house of his armour, and all that was found in his treasures: there was nothing in his house, nor in all his dominion, that Hezekiah shewed them not. Then came Isaiah the prophet unto king Hezekiah, and said unto him, What said these men? and from whence came they unto thee? And Hezekiah said, They are come from a far country, even from Babylon. And he said, What have they seen in thine house? And Hezekiah answered, All the things that are in mine house have they seen: there is nothing among my treasures that I have not shewed them. And Isaiah said unto Hezekiah, Hear the word of the Lord. Behold, the days come, that all that is in thine house, and that which thy fathers have laid up in store unto this day, shall be carried into Babylon: nothing shall be left, saith the Lord. And of thy sons that shall issue from thee, which thou shalt beget, shall they take away; and they shall be eunuchs in the palace of the king of Babylon. Then said Hezekiah unto Isaiah, Good is the word of the Lord which thou hast spoken. And he said, Is it not good, if peace and truth be in my days? And the rest of the acts of Hezekiah, and all his might, and how he made a pool, and a conduit, and brought water into the city, are they not written in the book of the chronicles of the kings of Judah? And Hezekiah slept with his fathers: and Manasseh his son reigned in his stead.

We find in the above passage that Hezekiah had an illness unto death, and he pleaded with God, who extended his life. We also find that he made a mistake and showed the enemy all that he had. Hezekiah probably would have been better off if he had accepted God's plan.

Often we as Christians pray for someone who is sick and then they die. When this happens, it can weaken or even destroy our faith. We may ask ourselves, "How much better is it to have the mind of Christ and pray the prayer of faith?" When my grandmother was pregnant with my Aunt Virginia, she had a stroke; and because of this, the doctors thought that my aunt was dead. Because they thought that she was dead, they were not careful when delivering her. They broke her back in the process, which led to her legs not having formed normally. My aunt spent her entire life in a wheelchair. In her lifetime, my aunt came to know Christ, and she had one of the most beautiful spirits that I have ever known. Everyone loved Aunt Virginia. She was able to overcome her handicap by operating a specialized switchboard that she had set up in her house. Eventually, she was earning more money than her brothers and sisters. Aunt Virginia was a very generous person and said that she would loan money to any of her nieces or nephews who wanted to go to medical school. I am a veterinarian today because I borrowed the money from her to go to college.

Years later, I received a letter from her, saying that she was ready to be with the Lord. When I read the letter, I took it to mean that she was saved and that when God calls her home, she is ready to be with him. A few days later, I received a call from my parents, who said that Aunt Virginia had cancer and was not expected to live. They asked me to remember her in my prayers. I tried as hard as I could, but I just could not pray. I felt just terrible about this because I loved her very, very much. A short time later, as I was in my office, God spoke to me and reminded me of her letter, and he wanted me to reread it. I did not have the letter with me, but I had read it enough that I knew what it said.

The Lord then spoke to me very clearly and said, "She has an illness unto death. She knows that she is going home, and she is ready."

I looked up at the Lord and said, "Lord, in the name of Jesus, please take her home." I then looked at the clock to see the time, and within an hour, I received a phone call from my parents. She died the very moment that I prayed to Jesus.

When we can come to the realization that for us to live is Christ and for us to die is gain, then death does not have a sting anymore. This is not to say that we will not miss those who die; we will miss them terribly.

My mother had cancer. One day I received a phone call that she had died; they revived her but did not expect her to live. My brother and I were able to catch a plane on which we had the last two seats. We got in at about one in the morning. My brother said that he was tired and was going to bed, but I went to see Mom. When I first walked in, I started telling her all about the family and everything that was going on. Then she said to me, "Will you be quiet?"

This was completely unlike my mother, who just did not say things like that.

She then said, "I want you to pray for me."

At that point, we stopped, had a word of prayer, and then continued with our conversation about the family. A short while later, she fell asleep and then went into a coma. I began to watch the EKG and saw that she was having heartbeats that were not supposed to be there. I realized that she was dying, and I told my sister that she had better call Dad since he wanted to be here. My mom was struggling to breathe while trying to stay alive. Finally, I looked at her and said, "Mom, I am going to say good night here, and I will say good morning when I see you on the other side." I then said to her, "Into the hands of the Lord I commit your soul. In Jesus's name, I release you." And that was it. She never took another breath. I could feel the presence of the Lord just sweep in and take her soul home.

A lady came into my office one day, and she was extremely distraught because her best friend had died. My wife, Jan, had met this friend at the church nursery and had become close friends with her also. This friend had five young children of which the youngest was a fifteen-month-old. We eventually left the church where we came to know her and started attending another church. During this time, the lady developed breast cancer. The church, evangelists, and practically everyone began praying for her. Eventually, she died.

Somehow, this just did not seem fair. A woman from the church came up to me and said, "What good does it do to pray?" She said, "I don't know how many times she was anointed with oil. I don't know how many people gave messages saying that she would be healed, and then she died."

Then I said to her, "Let me ask you a few questions. Did you spend time with her?"

She said, "Yes, I spent a lot of time with her because she was my best friend." I then said, "Let me ask you something else. What did you talk about?"

She said, "Once she received the diagnoses, all she could talk about was how sweet heaven was going to be and how she couldn't wait to get there."

I then asked her, "Do you not think that she had an illness unto death and that God had prepared her heart?"

She stopped, looked at me, and said, "I can't believe it. All this time she wanted to share with me how great heaven was and how through her dreams, God was revealing it to her. She was trying to minister to me about what heaven was like, and all I could do was say, 'Oh, do not talk like that. You are going to live.'" Then, with emotion, the woman said to me, "How much I have missed. If I had just been there to let her share the joys of the things that God was showing her."

An illness unto death can be difficult to accept; however, once we come to accept it and see where God is leading, no longer is it a defeat, but instead it becomes a victory. There is a time to be born and a time to die. One hundred years for one man is a good life. Twenty-five years for another one may be excellent.

As a pastor, I am often faced with the question, "Will you pray for me?"

My answer to this question is, "Yes, I can pray for you, but if I don't have the faith, then do you have the faith?"

There must be faith in there someplace. Sometimes God is going to heal, but there are certain things that must first happen before it comes about. God must first give us the grace to know the mind of Christ so that we know what to pray.

# FOR THE GLORY OF GOD

The third illness described in the Bible is *for the glory of God.* John 9:1–9 says:

> And as Jesus passed by, he saw a man which was blind from his birth. And his disciples asked him, saying, Master, who did sin, this man, or his parents, that he was born blind? Jesus answered, Neither hath this man sinned, nor his parents: but that the works of God should be made manifest in him. I must work the works of him that sent me, while it is day: the night cometh, when no man can work. As long as I am in the world, I am the light of the world. When he had thus spoken, he spat on the ground, and made clay of the spittle, and he anointed the eyes of the blind man with the clay, and said unto him, Go, wash in the pool of Silo'am (which is by interpretation, Sent.) He went his way therefore, and washed, and came seeing. The neighbors therefore, and they which before had seen him that he was blind, said, Is not this he that sat and begged? Some said, This is he: others said, He is like him: but he said, I am he.

We have already talked about the curse, judgment, and rebellion. Also, we talked about illnesses that are brought about because of sin. During the time period that we are studying, people believed that all illness was due to sin, even though Old Testament examples showed that illness causes could be for other reasons. We need to keep this in mind as people from different generations teach things that do not line up with scripture. We see in the passage above that illness can also be for God's glory.

John 11:1–6 says:

> Now a certain man was sick, named Lazarus, of Bethany, the town of Mary and her sister Martha. (It was that Mary which anointed the Lord with ointment, and wiped his feet with her hair, whose brother Lazarus was sick.) Therefore his sisters sent unto him, saying, Lord, behold, he whom thou lovest is sick. When Jesus heard that, he said, This sickness is not unto death, but for the glory of God, that the Son of God might be glorified thereby. Now Jesus loved Martha, and her sister, and Lazarus. When he had heard therefore that he was sick, he abode two days still in the same place where he was.

I had a young lady come to me one time who was having marital problems. She said that she called and left a message for her pastor to call her, and then she called and left a message for her lawyer too. Apparently, the lawyer called her back right away, but the pastor took longer to respond. She said that the result of her marriage was the pastor's fault because the lawyer called her back first. Let us be honest here: when we are hurting, we have no patience. We sometimes feel that if that pastor, deacon, or friend is not there to comfort us right away, then they must not love us. In other words, we want patience now. We see in the passage above that Jesus took a little time to respond.

John 11:7–44 says:

> Then after that saith he to his disciples, Let us go into Judea again. His disciples say unto him, Master, the Jews of late sought to stone thee; and goest thou thither again? Jesus answered, Are there not twelve hours in the day? If any man walk in the day, he stumbleth not, because he seeth the light of this world. But if a man walk in the night, he stumbleth, because there is no light in him. These things said he: and after that he saith unto them, Our friend Lazarus sleepeth; but I go, that I may awake him out of sleep. Then said his disciples, Lord, if he sleep, he shall do well. Howbeit Jesus spake of

his death: but they thought that he had spoken of taking of rest in sleep. Then said Jesus unto them plainly, Lazarus is dead. And I am glad for your sakes that I was not there, to the intent ye may believe; nevertheless let us go unto him. Then said Thomas, which is called Did'ymus, unto his fellow disciples, Let us also go, that we may die with him. Then when Jesus came, he found that he had lain in the grave four days already. Now Bethany was nigh unto Jerusalem, about fifteen furlongs off: and many of the Jews came to Martha and Mary, to comfort them concerning their brother. Then Martha, as soon as she heard that Jesus was coming, went and met him: but Mary sat still in the house. Then said Martha unto Jesus, Lord, if thou hadst been here, my brother had not died. But I know, that even now, whatsoever thou wilt ask of God, God will give it thee. Jesus saith unto her, Thy brother shall rise again. Martha saith unto him, I know that he shall rise again in the resurrection at the last day. Jesus said unto her, I am the resurrection, and the life: he that believeth in me, though he were dead, yet shall he live: and whosoever liveth and believeth in me shall never die. Believest thou this? She saith unto him, Yea, Lord: I believe that thou art the Christ, the Son of God, which should come into the world. And when she had so said, she went her way, and called Mary her sister secretly, saying, The Master is come, and calleth for thee. As soon as she heard that, she arose quickly, and came unto him. Now Jesus was not yet come into the town, but was in that place where Martha met him. The Jews then which were with her in the house, and comforted her, when they saw Mary, that she rose up hastily and went out, followed her, saying, She goeth unto the grave to weep there. Then when Mary was come where Jesus was, and saw him, she fell down at his feet, saying unto him, Lord, if thou hadst been here, my brother had not died. When Jesus therefore saw her weeping, and the Jews also weeping which came with her, he groaned in the spirit, and was troubled, and said, Where have ye laid him? They say unto him, Lord, come and see. Jesus wept.

Then said the Jews, Behold how he loved him! And some of them said, Could not this man, which opened the eyes of the blind, have caused that even this man should not have died? Jesus therefore again groaning in himself cometh to the grave. It was a cave, and a stone lay upon it. Jesus said, Take ye away the stone. Martha, the sister of him that was dead, saith unto him, Lord, by this time he stinketh: for he hath been dead four days. Jesus saith unto her, Said I not unto thee, that, if thou wouldest believe, thou shouldest see the glory of God? Then they took away the stone from the place where the dead was laid. And Jesus lifted up his eyes, and said, Father, I thank thee that thou hast heard me. And I knew that thou hearest me always: but because of the people which stand by I said it, that they may believe that thou hast sent me. And when he thus had spoken, he cried with a loud voice, Lazarus, come forth. And he that was dead came forth, bound hand and foot with graveclothes; and his face was bound about with a napkin. Jesus saith unto them, Loose him, and let him go.

We learn in the passages above that Lazarus' illness was not unto death but was for the glory of God. When Jesus went to Lazarus' grave, not only did Lazarus stink, but so did the stuff that was on him; however, he did not stink when he came forth. This is the power of God to clean it up. Also described in the passages above is a blind man who was born blind so that when Jesus healed him, God would be glorified. God used both healings to bring many people to Jesus.

Our second son was born with both feet turned the same direction, which inhibited him from learning to walk. Our doctor said that he would like to refer us to a specialist so that his foot could be fixed. As I got ready to go to bed the night before we were to see the specialist, I was praying, and the Lord said to me, "Go back to John 9:1–7, where it speaks of the man who was born blind for my glory. Your son also was born this way for my glory."

I then said, "Lord, I thank you that his foot is going to turn in the correct position."

The next morning, when I got up, both of his feet were in the normal position. God allowed our son to be born this way and then healed him for God's glory.

When something tragic happens, whether it be an illness, an automobile accident, or whatever it is that appears to be a disaster in our lives, stop and ask God, "Is there something in this that will bring glory to you?" Not always, but many times, there is. If there is, God will reveal it to you and use you to bring glory to that situation. This can be a powerful testimony to someone who needs it.

At this point, I would like to share with you my experience of having to have a heart catheterization. One day, when I was fifty years old, I began having severe chest pains. I was not born ignorant, and being in the medical profession, I knew what was going on; however, I did not have time to have a heart attack. It simply did not fit into my schedule. At the time, my dad was not doing well, and we had made plans to fly our family to North Dakota to see him. We planned to go during Memorial Day weekend, so I did not say anything to Jan or anybody else about my pains.

I discovered that when I would lie down, the pains would go away, so I decided that I would be fine if I just kept doing that. One Saturday afternoon, I took my family to a lake that was just south of Dallas. We had a very relaxing good time, but as we were driving back, I began having very severe chest pains. The closer we got to Dallas, the more severe the pains became.

When we finally got to the final stretch of road leading into Dallas, I was in such pain that it felt like a chain was strapped across and squeezing my chest. I started sweating, and the sweat was just pouring off my face. At that point, I knew that I could not go home but needed to get to the hospital. As I made the interchange onto the highway leading to Baylor Hospital, Jan finally looked at me and said, "Where are you going."

I then replied, "I think that I'm having a heart attack, and I'm heading for Baylor Hospital."

She said, "You need to pull over and let me drive."

"No, I know how to get there. I'll pull up to the emergency entrance and get out, then you can park the car," I said. I also asked her to call my doctor at home as soon as we arrived.

As I walked into the emergency entrance and up to the receptionist's desk, I became aware that she was ignoring everyone, including me, because she was on a personal phone call. Meanwhile, one of the nurses came walking up to me and said, "You don't look too good. Please have a seat, and we will be with you in a minute." Then she looked back at me once more and said, "What is going on? You do not look so good."

"I think I am having a heart attack," I told her.

Then she said, "Sit down right here, and I will take your blood pressure." When she did, it was two hundred and forty-something over about one hundred fifty or sixty—it was just outrageous. She said, "Do not move, I am going to go get wheels." I told her that I could walk, and she immediately replied, "I said do not move." She came back with a wheelchair, told me to get in it, and wheeled me to a room where there were two doctors and three nurses waiting.

They slapped an EKG on me and took my blood pressure, which was sky high. Everyone was in a total panic. Next, they put a nitroglycerine patch on my chest, a nitroglycerine tablet under my tongue, and worked on me for about forty-five minutes. By this time, my chest pains were relieving, and things were beginning to straighten out. I then said to the medical team, "You guys won't do a catheterization tonight. It is the weekend, so you will not do it until Monday anyway. I will just go home and sleep in my waterbed where I will be much more comfortable."

Then the nurse said to me, "I am going to get your wife. She seemed to be awfully concerned." When my wife came in, the nurse said to her, "Take all of his clothes because if he is leaving this hospital, he is going out of here naked."

To make a long story short, they put me in the ICU, and when the doctor came in, he said, "I have got good news, bad news, and good news." He said, "The bad news is that you have been doing everything that you can to try and have a heart attack. The good news is that you have not had one yet, and that we are going to do everything we can to try and prevent it."

They left me in the ICU, would not let me get out of bed or have any phone calls or messages, and they expected for me to lie still and be quiet. On Sunday night, the doctors came in to let me know that they were going to do a catheter on Monday and then bypass surgery on Tuesday. I said, "No, you are going to do the catheter and bypass surgery on the same day, even if that means waiting until Tuesday. I am not going to lie here for twenty-four hours with a catheter in my leg."

When they came in on Monday morning, they said, "Who are you?" I said, "I'm Ernie Martin."

They said, "No, that is not what we're talking about. Who are you? What kind of VIP are you?" They then told me, "This does not happen at Baylor Hospital, but the six top cardiologists are on your case and have been reviewing it. You will have your catheter today while the surgeon is waiting to do your surgery right after."

"Okay," I said.

When they came to get me for the catheterization, the doctor said to me, "You may think that you are just getting a catheter and a little angioplasty, and then you are going home today. Let me tell you this: you are not. Six of our cardiologists have reviewed your case. You have at least three major blood vessels that are blocked close to 90 percent. You will have bypass surgery today." When he saw my wife in the waiting room, he told her the same thing and told her to be prepared to wait for six to eight hours until the surgery is over.

At this point, my blood pressure was still bouncing into the 230s, my color was kind of gray, and I was not doing so well. When they took me in, the doctor said, "Do you want a sedative?"

"No, I want to watch it," I said.

"Okay, you can watch it if you want to," he said.

When they got ready to put in the dye, he said, "Okay, now take a look and be prepared to get a great big hot flash."

It did not seem to do that much to me. The next thing I knew, this doctor started jumping around. He said, "It is impossible, impossible! We have just seen a miracle! This fifty-year-old man has no plaque in his vessels at all!"

Next they decided to try the other side, and it was the same thing. My blood pressure then immediately had gone back to normal, and my color came back to pink. He looked at me and said, "This is a miracle! God has cleaned out your vessels."

One of the cardiologists came to our church and testified. He said, "I have prayed all my life to see a miracle, and I saw a miracle. This man's vessels were clean. Six top cardiologists did not miss it. God healed him." I believe that it was because the whole church was praying for me as well as other people, and God heard their prayers. God chose for his glory to touch and heal me.

# ILLNESS OF CHASTISEMENT CAUSED BY SIN

Continuing with our exploration of illnesses found in the Bible, let us now learn about the illness of chastisement caused by sin. Another type of chastisement discussed in the Bible can be found in Hebrews and is a "molding" type of chastisement. What I mean by this is that it is the type of chastisement that makes us into the image of Christ. The type of chastisement that we are going to learn about in this lesson is that which is a result of sin and can produce illnesses.

John 5:1–9 says:

> After this there was a feast of the Jews; and Jesus went up to Jerusalem. Now there is at Jerusalem by the sheep market a pool, which is called in the Hebrew tongue Bethes'da, having five porches. In these lay a great multitude of impotent folk, of blind, halt, withered, waiting for the moving of the water. For an angel went down at a certain season into the pool, and troubled the water: whosoever then first after the troubling of the water stepped in was made whole of whatsoever disease he had. And a certain man was there, which had an infirmity thirty and eight years. When Jesus saw him lie, and knew that he had been now a long time in that case, he saith unto him, Wilt thou be made whole? The impotent man answered him, Sir, I have no man, when the water is troubled, to put me into the pool: but while I am coming, another steppeth down

before me. Jesus saith unto him, Rise, take up thy bed, and walk. And immediately the man was made whole, and took up his bed, and walked: and on the same day was the sabbath.

An important thing that I would like to point out about the pool, as described in the passage above, is that it is surrounded by nothing but sick people; however, amongst all of them, Jesus picks out just one. I think that this is an important passage to keep in mind because it demonstrates how he was doing the will of his Father. He did not just heal everybody. He walked away from the pool with multitudes of people not having been healed.

So many times when we speak with people who don't believe in healing or don't want to accept the fact that God divinely intervenes and heals without using a doctor, we hear them say, "Well, then, if you have all that power, why don't you just go to the hospital, pray for everyone who's there, and empty the hospital?"

I do not have that power, and when I try to explain this to them, I am usually confronted with a defense against God's ability to divinely intervene.

Continuing on this note, I would like to briefly skip over to the book of Mark and discuss some passages.

Mark 16:15–18 says:

And he said unto them, Go ye into all the world, and preach the gospel to every creature. He that believeth and is baptized shall be saved; but he that believeth not shall be damned. And these signs shall follow them that believe; In my name shall they cast out devils; they shall speak with new tongues; they shall take up serpents; and if they drink any deadly thing, it shall not hurt them; they shall lay hands on the sick, and they shall recover.

The passage above tells us that we must not only believe in Christ to be saved but that we must also believe in the signs that follow. In other words, we must believe that God performs miracles today or it is probably not going to happen. We have learned that Jesus could perform very few miracles in his hometown because unbelief was so great. When he went in and raised up the little girl who was dead, we learned that he first put out all the people that did not believe.

From the above passages in Mark, as well as those which we just read from John, we learn that having religion and being religious is just not enough. We must also have faith and turn our lives over to Christ.

Another point that I would like to touch on is that there are two ways to get to heaven. If there were not, then there would be no salvation for any of us. Okay now you are saying, "This guy has really flipped out!" I am serious when I say that Christ was the law completed; he came not to destroy the law but to fulfill the law through love. Jesus was resurrected because he kept the law, and if he had not, then there would not be that means of salvation; therefore, none of us would have salvation. Sometimes we forget that Jesus became total flesh and blood. He had to keep the law as the son of man and not as the divine Son of God.

When Jesus took on the form of man, there had to be a means by which he could be resurrected, and keeping the law was his means. So when I say that there is another way to get to heaven, what I am referring to is keeping the law.

Jesus kept the law while in the form of man, and therefore, he showed us that man could. As we begin to understand this, we can then begin to understand the power of what Jesus Christ did; he kept the law so that God could raise him up. God did raise him up after Jesus took our place on the cross and died for our sins. Jesus was resurrected by faith, believing that if he kept the law, God could and would raise him from the dead.

One question I would like to ask is, "Do you know what *hell* really means?" When the Bible says that every knee shall bow, and every tongue shall confess that Jesus Christ is the Son of God, it is referring to the time of meeting God at death. Those who did not know God before death will be cast into the lake of fire, which is eternal damnation in hell. God will cast them out of his presence after they have made that confession because they made it after they died instead of before they died. The only time in his life that Jesus was separated from his Father was when he took on himself the sins of man on the cross. His Father took the Holy Spirit from him, and he died alone.

This is what caused him to be in such anguish while in the Garden of Gethsemane. Jesus paid the penalty for sin when he died, descended into hell, and was separated from his Father. Then he was resurrected by the Holy Spirit.

As I was reading some passages in Hebrews the other night, God really began to speak to me. He was telling me that when we look at marriage, and we look at God and the Holy Spirit, we see an essence of the same relationship. When we are married to our wife or husband, we become one flesh through the event of our sexual relationship. Similarly, when we accept Jesus Christ as our Lord and Savior, we become the bride. At that point, he comes in to live in us, and we become one with him. Oneness and joy develop, which is not unlike the joy once felt during our salvation. It is a feeling of wanting to let the world know your joy, while at the same time not caring what the world thinks.

At the very moment when we accepted Christ, we were sinless. It may have only lasted ten seconds, but we were sinless. When we look at God in this light, are we walking in that fellowship with God today? Are we walking, not caring what the world thinks or what anybody else says about our faith? Have we found oneness with God or are we drifting from our first love? As I was reading Hebrews, and God was speaking to me, I began to think, *God, this is where we need to come. We need to come unto you so that we can have oneness with you, just like Jesus Christ, so that we can have constant communication with you.* If we could do this, then we could understand some of the grief and sorrow that Jesus went through in the Garden of Gethsemane. We could understand how Jesus felt when he cried out, "My God! My God! Why have you forsaken me?" The true torment of hell will be the separation felt by those who have recognized God and then have been cast out by him. This should really motivate us to have compassion and concern for those who are lost.

John 5:10–15 says:

> The Jews therefore said unto him that was cured, It is the sabbath day: it is not lawful for thee to carry thy bed. He answered them, He that made me whole, the same said

unto me, Take up thy bed, and walk. Then asked they him, What man is that which said unto thee, Take up thy bed, and walk? And he that was healed wist not who it was: for Jesus had conveyed himself away, a multitude being in that place. Afterward Jesus findeth him in the temple, and said unto him, Behold, thou art made whole: sin no more, lest a worse thing come unto thee. The man departed, and told the Jews that it was Jesus, which had made him whole.

The inference in the passage above is that the man was in the state that he was in because of sin. Jesus told him not to sin anymore unless a worse thing come upon him.

James 5:14–16 says:

Is any sick among you? let him call for the elders of the church; and let them pray over him, anointing him with oil in the name of the Lord: and the prayer of faith shall save the sick, and the Lord shall raise him up; and if he have committed sins, they shall be forgiven him. Confess your faults one to another, and pray one for another, that ye may be healed. The effectual fervent prayer of a righteous man availeth much.

Right after I was saved and filled with the Holy Spirit, I became extremely sick. I kept praying about it, and nothing was happening. Finally, in my immaturity, I said to God, "Have I lost my touch?" Before that, it seemed as though every time I prayed for someone, they became well. People were coming to me by word of mouth from others who had been healed, and God was healing them through me. It appeared that I was the only one who could not get well.

Finally the Lord spoke to me through verse 16 above, "Confess your faults one to another, and pray one for another, that you may be healed." He was telling me that I had sinned against a brother. He told me to go to him and ask him to pray for me, and he would hear it. So I did just that, and God instantly healed me.

Personally I feel that this is one area of the Scriptures that is overlooked. When people come forward for prayer, they want prayer. If they are sick, they want to be healed through prayer; however, one thing that is forgotten is that we must first deal with the sin that is in our life. I have shared the testimony of the two women who would not forgive their ex-husbands and remained sick until they finally confessed it. Then God healed them. This is one of those things that we must come to grips with.

First Corinthians 11:23–34 says:

> For I have received of the Lord that which also I delivered unto you, That the Lord Jesus, the same night in which he was betrayed, took bread: and when he had given thanks, he brake it, and said, Take, eat; this is my body, which is broken for you: this do in remembrance of me. After the same manner also he took the cup, when he had supped, saying, This cup is the new testament in my blood: this do ye, as oft as ye drink it, in remembrance of me. For as often as ye eat this bread, and drink this cup, ye do show the Lord's death till he come. Wherefore whosoever shall eat this bread, and drink this cup of the Lord, unworthily, shall be guilty of the body and blood of the Lord. But let a man examine himself, and so let him eat of that bread, and drink of that cup. For he that eateth and drinketh unworthily, eateth and drinketh damnation to himself, not discerning the Lord's body. For this cause many are weak and sickly among you, and many sleep. For if we would judge ourselves, we should not be judged. But when we are judged, we are chastened of the Lord, that we should not be condemned with the world. Wherefore, my brethren, when ye come together to eat, tarry one for another. And if any man hunger, let him eat at home; that ye come not together unto condemnation. And the rest will I set in order when I come.

The passages above tell us that it is a profoundly serious thing to partake of Holy Communion. It clearly states that there are many people who are sick and even some who are dead because they did not realize the significance of it.

This scripture reminds me that one of the nice things about being a pastor in a small church, as I once was, is that I was able to devote an entire service to Holy Communion. We took this event very, very literally, and we felt that we needed to give everyone a chance to get right with God prior to receiving communion. I feel that too much of the time today, Holy Communion becomes a routine in our own lives, and we don't always stop to consider the significance of it. The Bible says very clearly that if you take unworthily, then judgment will come.

The feelings that may be occurring in some of us because of these lessons are something that I would like to speak about. Some of us may be thinking, *I've been sick a lot lately, and I can't seem to get well. I must have a sin, but I don't know what it is.* I guarantee you that if you have sinned, then you know what it is. You may have buried it and tried to cover it up, but it does not go away.

When God called me into the ministry, he said, "I do not want any skeletons in the clothes closet. Search your heart."

"No, Lord, there are no skeletons in my clothes closet," was my reply.

He then said to me, "The man of God who is going to preach must be above and beyond reproach. So what might not be a skeleton for somebody else may be a skeleton for you. You need to look again."

There was something that just kept lingering in my mind. Once, when we had bought a house, the contractor had not done what he was supposed to do; so my lawyer told me to hold back part of the money. We did just that, which is what we were supposed to legally do. God said, "No. You need to pay him."

I said to the Lord, "I do not even have the money to pay him, but if that is what you want, then that is what I will do." This had been going on for about three years with the work not having been completed and us not paying him. Then, one day, I called him up and told him that I was going to pay him.

The part that was left unpaid was on an interest-free note, so when I got ready to go pay him, the Lord said, "If he asks for your coat, give him your shirt."

When I got there and presented the payment, he said to me, "I have to have interest on that."

I said to him, "Sir, the note said that there was no interest." Keeping in mind that the Lord told me to give him my shirt, I then said, "Okay, but you are going to have to hold the check because I don't have the money." Consequently, the Lord then provided me with enough money coming into the office on that day to pay for the interest. I did not know it at the time, so I told him that I would call him the next day and let him know when he could cash the check. I called him, he cashed the check, and he was paid for not only the note but also for the interest. They then came and fixed the house, but they ended up spending three times as much money because the uncompleted areas had begun to deteriorate to the point at which a lot of the materials needed to be replaced. For example, the paint on the shutters was so poor that right away it began chipping, and when we asked them to repaint, they never did.

By this time, the shutters had completely rotted out. Therefore, the shutters had to be completely replaced. This whole ordeal ended up costing them a whole lot more than if they had just done what they were supposed to in the beginning. But you see, God said to me, "I do not care what they do. You said that you would pay them that money, so you must pay it." God asks us to do things in love, regardless of what other people do. Sometimes doing what God tells us to do is not in conjunction with the legal and other advice that we may receive; however, we must not forget that the right way is God's way. It is amazing what changes will occur in our lives when we listen to and follow God's will.

Hebrews 12:1–17 says:

> Wherefore, seeing we also are compassed about with so great a cloud of witnesses, let us lay aside every weight, and the sin which doth so easily beset us, and let us run with patience the race that is set before us, looking unto Jesus the author and finisher of our faith; who for the joy that was set before him endured the cross, despising the shame, and is set down at the right hand of the throne of God. For consider him that endured such contradiction of sinners against himself, lest ye be wearied and faint in your minds. Ye have not yet resisted unto blood, striving against sin. And ye have forgotten the exhortation which speaketh unto you as unto children, My son, despise not thou the chastening of the Lord, nor faint

when thou art rebuked of him: for whom the Lord loveth he chasteneth, and scourgeth every son whom he receiveth. If ye endure chastening, God dealeth with you as with sons; for what son is he whom the father chasteneth not? But if ye be without chastisement, whereof all are partakers, then are ye bastards, and not sons. Furthermore, we have had fathers of our flesh which corrected us, and we gave them reverence: shall we not much rather be in subjection unto the Father of spirits, and live? For they verily for a few days chastened us after their own pleasure; but he for our profit, that we might be partakers of his holiness. Now no chastening for the present seemeth to be joyous, but grievous: nevertheless, afterward it yieldeth the peaceable fruit of righteousness unto them which are exercised thereby. Wherefore lift up the hands which hang down, and the feeble knees; and make straight paths for your feet, lest that which is lame be turned out of the way; but let it rather be healed. Follow peace with all men, and holiness, without which no man shall see the Lord: looking diligently lest any man fail of the grace of God; lest any root of bitterness springing up trouble you, and thereby many be defiled; lest there be any fornicator, or profane person, as Esau, who for one morsel of meat sold his birthright. For ye know how that afterward, when he would have inherited the blessing, he was rejected: for he found no place of repentance, though he sought it carefully with tears.

This scripture has a double meaning of chastisement. Some of the chastisement that it describes is that of judgment due to sin and some is molding where there is no sin.

Just as in the passage above, the Lord is asking us to also look to the joy that awaits us. Think of how much better it would be to arrive at heaven and be greeted with, "Well done, thou faithful servant" than, "Well, servant, we are letting you in, but that is about all."

I used to think that it was wrong and that it was prideful to want an abundant entrance into heaven, but Paul said that he had an abundant entrance awaiting him. He said that when he got to heaven there would be a lot of people there to greet him who would be thrilled to see him coming. I can only hope that it is the same for me. I hope that when they see me coming that they go get all of my friends and say, "Ernie Martin is coming! Let us go down to the pearly gates to meet him and welcome him home!"

In order to walk in the presence of God, we must put on the righteousness of Christ and become holy; however, if we keep sin in our life, and we keep practicing sin, then there won't be a place for Christ in our life. A piece of scripture that I would advise everyone to spend some time meditating on is verse 11 above: "Now no chastening for the present seems to be joyous, but grievous: nevertheless, afterward it yields the peaceable fruit of righteousness unto them which are exercised thereby."

One thing that I would like for all of us to understand is that God doesn't expect for those of us at the start of our learning who are chastened by him to say, "Oh give me another lick. God, this feels good." He knows that we are human, and he says that it does not appear to be joyous but appears to be very grievous. In other words, he gets down where we are. If we can only learn to be honest with God and see that, then we can have a breakthrough. It doesn't work for us to say, "Praise the Lord" and think, *God, I am really mad at you, for I thought that being a Christian was supposed to be full of joy and not chastisement.*

To illustrate this point, I would like to describe a scenario, which goes as such: a Christian scientist, a Catholic, and a Baptist died and ended up in hell. The Baptist said, "I blew it. I thought that I was saved, but I just flat blew it."

The Catholic said, "I do not have anything to worry about. They are going to pray me out of here."

The Christian scientist said, "I am not here, I am not here, I am not here, I am not here."

I put forth this picture only to illustrate that this is exactly what some of us are doing. Some Christians are doing the same thing when they tell themselves, "I am not sick, I am not sick, I am not sick, I am not sick. Everything is fine, everything is fine, everything is fine, everything is fine." No, it is not; everything is not fine. God knows your thoughts, so say your thoughts and get it out. Then confess to him and ask for his forgiveness. He says very clearly, "Make sacrificial praise with your lips." The greatest victory in our life is when we become honest with God and quit trying to put on that we are something we are not.

If there is one thing that I can go back to, it is, "Thank God my name is written in the book of life." When I go back to this point and start again, I am getting down to the real nitty-gritty where no matter what else happens to me, eventually, I am going home. I can then start dealing with the devil and say to him, "Devil, you can bring all of hell against me, and it will not make any difference because if you kill me, it will be a reward. I will be out of this place and in heaven." This is really what I want anyway, but God is just not doing it.

This was Job's problem also. He wished that God would release his hold so that Satan could just take his life and he could die. It appears the only time we want the Lord to come is when we are faced with problems. When everything is going well, we tend to say, "Whoa, Lord, just hold off a little while. I've got some friends who need to be saved. I am enjoying life right now, Lord, so hold off a little bit."

In contrast, when the world begins to cave in, we say, "Hey, Jesus, hurry up and come right now." Aren't we fickle? I just do not know how God puts up with us; thank God he does. He knows that sometimes we do not want to pray, that sometimes we do not want to worship him, and that sometimes we do not want to read his Word, but he loves us anyway.

One of the hardest things for a mother is when her child comes to her and says, "I hate you." I would doubt that there are many mothers who have not had this happen to them. Hearing the words "I hate you" may have broken your heart and pierced you, but it did not make you stop loving. Our heavenly Father is so much greater. He looks down on us and says, "I know where you're at. I know you are hurting. I know you're struggling, and I'm going to heat things up so that you can come into the glorious victory of walking in the Spirit."

We can remember back to Shadrach, Meshach, and Abednego and how the fire was heated up seven times hotter than it had ever been heated. Not only was the fire seven times hotter, but they put coats on the three men to ensure that they would catch on fire. The fire was so hot that the guys who threw them in were killed. The king then looked in and saw not three people but four; Jesus was walking around in there. The only thing that was burnt off was the ropes that bound them. I, myself, have fought fires in which my eyebrows were completely singed off, and the hair on my head and the back of my hand was singed. I will tell you what. If there is a big prairie fire going, then you will be down there with gunnysacks, trying to beat the flames out. If you do not, then somebody's house is going to get burned down. You must keep on fighting.

I definitely don't want chastisement, but I've learned one thing about when it does come, and that is to say, "Oh God, finish your work because I don't want to go through this again." In other words, do not make it short, but please finish it all now so that it can be done.

When we first started these lessons, I made the statement, "The number one problem we have is taking people off of the cross." With our children, we are especially guilty of this. We need to turn them over to God and say, "God, whatever it takes, they are in your hands, and we trust you with them." We must let them suffer so that God can have his full work with them.

I think that the passage above makes a very profound statement when it talks about Esau. When Esau came in, he was hungry; if Jacob had been a good brother, he would have offered him that bowl of stew. Jacob's name means deceitful. When Jacob wrestled with Jesus, Jesus said to him, "Who are you?"

He said to Jesus, "I'm Jacob."

Jesus then said to him, "That's who you are, the deceiver."

Jacob realized he was wrestling with the Lord and said, "I'm not going to let you go."

The Lord then said to him, "I'm going to change your name." This is when Jacob was converted.

Another beautiful part of this story happened when Joseph was in Egypt. During the time when they were going to have to take Benjamin back to Egypt, different names were mentioned in this story, such as Jacob and Israel. When Jacob was in the flesh, he used the name Jacob; but when he was walking by faith, he used the name Israel. If you read the story and keep this in mind, you can really see the beauty of it. Jacob would walk by faith and then slip back into the flesh, using the name Israel and then Jacob. Repeatedly he used the names, going back and forth. One of the things that really excites me about this story is that we can really see how we are.

Years ago, I used to read my Bible differently than I do today; I used to have all kinds of study guides to go along with it. One day, the Lord spoke to me and said, "It is line on line and precept on precept. I want you to start at the book of Genesis and read through the whole Bible."

I usually read through the Bible two to three times per year. After having received this message, I noticed that each time I went back to the beginning of the Bible to read it, God started giving me a central theme that carried through from Genesis to Revelation. Each time that I read the Bible, I receive a new theme that he teaches me. This is the most exciting thing because I am not only reading this central theme in Genesis, but I am also reading it in Matthew, Isaiah, and all the other books too.

I am not saying that this is the way you should study the Bible, but I just wanted to share with you the excitement of how I am studying it. One time, while reading, God said to me, "I want for you to put yourself into the shoes of each one of the people who you are learning about."

I thought to myself, *Great! I'm going to try to find a way to identify with Paul and those great people.* So I get right to it, and the first man who I read about is Cain. I found out that I was more like Cain than I will ever be like Abel. When I began to read it and put myself in their places, I began to understand it. If we stop and think about this for a minute, you bring your offering to God, and he rejects it; and then that weaselly little brother of yours brings his offering to God, and God accepts his. If you have brothers and sisters, then you know from where I am coming. "How dare God accept that little brother's offering over mine." This is just like the things that happen in our lives when we put ourselves in their place and see that sometimes we react more like Cain than Abel.

In Hebrews, it talks about sons being chastised, "Whom God loves he chastises." One of the ways God chastises is through illness, which is not the only way but just one of the ways. The impotent man at the pool of Bethesda was healed by Jesus, who told him, "Go and sin no more unless a worse thing come upon you" with the implication being that his affliction was the result of sin. In James 5:14–17, we learned that if we have sin, it will be forgiven when we are anointed with oil and are prayed for. Also, it admonishes us to confess our sins to one another that we may be healed.

Hebrews 12:1 says:

> Wherefore, seeing we also are compassed about with so great a cloud of witnesses, let us lay aside every weight, and the sin which doth so easily beset us, and let us run with patience the race that is set before us.

The sin that we most commonly overlook, which is what the entire book of Hebrews is about, is unbelief. Frankly, this is the greatest sin that we have in our lives; we just do not believe God. It is not really the sins that we commit, not that we do not all have our struggles, but our biggest sin of all is that we do not believe God. Hebrews is about faith but more about unbelief. This is the sin that keeps weighing us down. Our next biggest struggle is also mentioned in the verse above, and that is, "Let us run with patience the race that is set before us." We do not run with patience; we want to be spiritual immediately. We are not patient with God to let God work it out in our life so that it is lasting. There is a difference. You can have some great things happening in your life and suddenly think that you are God's "man of the hour," but it will not last. The slow trials and tribulations that mold us are the ones that will last.

I cannot tell you how many times this one scripture has been the single thing that has kept me going. He is the author of my faith and the finisher of my faith. There have been times when I have said, "Lord, it doesn't look like I'm going to make it to the end." The Word tells us that once we have started it, what you begin, you will complete. So we are just going to have to trust him that he knows what he is doing because I sure don't. One thing that we should all keep in mind when things get really tough and it seems as though our world has come crashing down is that there is a day when we are going to stand in his presence. He will look down on us and say, "Well done, my faithful servants."

Hebrews 12:2–3 says:

> Looking unto Jesus the author and finisher of our faith; who for the joy that was set before him endured the cross, despising the shame, and is set down at the right hand of the throne of God. For consider him that endured such contradiction of sinners against himself, lest ye be wearied and faint in your minds.

It appears everyone is telling us to forget the mind and pay attention to the heart; however, our struggle is in the mind. What we must do is relearn to think. Negative thinking is one of the reasons why marriages get into trouble. To turn a marriage around and save it, you must teach people how to rethink. If you have a marriage and want it to keep going, be sure that you guard your thinking. It is easy to become negative. It just seems to happen. To stay positive can be difficult when things seem to be going against you.

When people come to me with marital problems, the first thing I do is ask them to start each day by listing a good thing about their mate. At first, it is easy. But to think of a new and different thing each day eventually becomes more and more challenging. They must start looking and searching for all the positive things. The result is that their thinking is changed from negative. Because they are so busy looking and focusing on the positive, there is no longer any time for the negative. We can do the same thing with God.

Hebrews 12:4–5 says:

Ye have not yet resisted unto blood, striving against sin. And ye have forgotten the exhortation which speaketh unto you as unto children, My son, despise not thou the chastening of the Lord, nor faint when thou art rebuked of him.

The passage above tells us that we must not become angry or bitter against the chastisement of the Lord. He is not looking at us as we are right now. He is looking at us in the image of his Son, Jesus Christ. He knows what it takes to get us from where we are to where we need to be. We can think of it as God being the Potter, and we are being the clay. The clay that resists the Potter is going to have a real struggle in becoming the vessel that the Potter wants it to be; however, the clay that lets the Lord be in charge will eventually become a beautiful vessel—God's image of us is in his Son, Jesus Christ. He wants to make us like Him.

If we go back and read our Bibles again, we will discover how Christ learned obedience; we find that it was through suffering. He became what his Father wanted him to be through suffering. Christ took on man's body with all its limitations, and he felt all our desires and hungers. For his Spirit to overcome the weaknesses of the flesh, he had to suffer to be molded into the perfect sacrifice. This is what the passage above is talking about, and it is also one of the chastening that we fail to understand in the scripture.

The scripture says, "Let the chastening of the Lord have its full and complete work." This is an awfully hard thing and is the area that we will struggle the most with. When we have one of these afflictions, we do not want to say to the Lord, "Lord, deliver me." We want to say, "Lord, give me the grace." The Apostle Paul was given a messenger of Satan to buffet him, and God told him that his grace was sufficient. He was not going to heal Paul, take the messenger away, or stop it so that Paul would not be exalted above his measure. God may allow something to happen in our lives and do the same thing.

Hebrews 12:6–11 says:

> For whom the Lord loveth he chasteneth, and scourgeth every son whom he receiveth. If ye endure chastening, God dealeth with you as with sons; for what son is he whom the father chasteneth not? But if ye be without chastisement, whereof all are partakers, then are ye bastards, and not sons. Furthermore, we have had fathers of our flesh which corrected us, and we gave them reverence: shall we not much rather be in subjection unto the Father of spirits, and live? For they verily for a few days chastened us after their own pleasure; but he for our profit, that we might be partakers of his holiness. Now no chastening for the present seemeth to be joyous, but

grievous: nevertheless, afterward it yieldeth the peaceable fruit of righteousness unto them which are exercised thereby.

I can imagine that every one of us has, at some time, prayed to God to make us just like Jesus. Do we know what we prayed when we prayed it? Most of us do not know what we pray when we pray. Sometimes we pray a prayer because it is really what we want, but we do not know how God is going to get us there. It may be a good prayer, but we just do not know the consequences of praying it unless we get a foresight that God is sovereign. When we can come to understand that God is sovereign, then it is a lot easier to go with the flow. We then can understand that it is he who has everything in his hands, and nothing can happen to us unless he allows it. He will never leave nor forsake us, but he will always be with us. God knows where we are and how to get us to where we need to be with each prayer that we pray.

I would like to briefly skip over to the book of Isaiah and discuss a few key passages.

Isaiah 55:1–2 says:

> Ho, every one that thirsteth, come ye to the waters, and he that hath no money; come ye, buy, and eat; yea, come, buy wine and milk without money and without price. Wherefore do ye spend money for that which is not bread? and your labor for that which satisfieth not? hearken diligently unto me, and eat ye that which is good, and let your soul delight itself in fatness.

The passage above tells us that there is no money that can buy Christ; he is priceless. Also it tells us to delight ourselves in the Word, and it says that it is one thing we cannot overeat on. We should make our souls fat with the Word.

Isaiah 55:8–9 says:

> For my thoughts are not your thoughts, neither are your ways my ways, saith the Lord. For as the heavens are higher than the earth, so are my ways higher than your ways, and my thoughts than your thoughts.

In Proverbs 3:5-6, the Lord is telling us to lean not to our own understanding but in all ways acknowledge him, and he will direct us. Hebrews 12:12–17 says:

> Wherefore lift up the hands which hang down, and the feeble knees; and make straight paths for your feet, lest that which is lame be turned out of the way; but let it rather be healed. Follow peace with all men, and holiness, without which no man shall see the Lord: looking diligently lest any man fail of the grace of God; lest any root of bitterness springing up trouble you, and thereby many be defiled; lest there be any fornicator, or profane person, as Esau, who for one morsel of meat sold his birthright. For ye know how that afterward, when he would have inherited the blessing, he was rejected: for he found no place of repentance, though he sought it carefully with tears.

In the book of Ephesians, it says to put on the armor of God, prepare to stand, and then stand. Hebrews states that the chastisement is coming, so get up and make a straight path for the throne of grace. We also learn to follow peace and holiness with all men because without it, we will not see the light. It is easy for a root of bitterness to get hold of us, even though we have the right to be bitter. God did not say that we could not be bitter, but he did say that his people rise above it because they learn to forgive. Esau did not realize the value of forgiveness. I will not deny that his brother Jacob was a sneaky character who should have loved his brother enough to give him the stew, but instead he found a way to get the birthright. It showed us how fleshly that Esau was. We must be careful, for if we are in the same boat, we could, in a moment's time, make a foolish mistake because we are walking in the flesh and not in the Spirit.

I have always wondered what would have happened if Jacob's mother had not worked out a way for him to steal the blessing. God was going to give it to Jacob. How would God have done it if Jacob's mother had not of worked out a way to make the venison, put the goat skin on Jacob, send him in to his father, and tell him to lie? He got it by deception, but God did not take it away from him.

If we look at David and Bathsheba, Solomon became God's choice for king. Look at the rebuke that he gave David when he said to him, "Did you not have enough wives that you had to kill a man and steal his wife?" Did God really want David to marry Bathsheba? He did not want him to marry her in that way. If we rewrote some of these stories, such as David and his adultery with Bathsheba and the murder of her husband, and if we put that in the headlines today, would we say that this is a man after God's heart? We all respect and admire David.

Another thing that we fail to realize is that Manasseh was the most evil and wicked king of Israel, and God let him reign for fifty-two years. It was longer than any other king. If we read the end of the story of Chronicles, we find that Manasseh repented, and God allowed him to reign fifty-two years so that he could repent. God's thoughts and ways are so high above ours that we just cannot comprehend them. When I stop and see God's mercy and grace, it gives me hope. I fall so short of God's plan for my life that, at times, I feel as though I am a hopeless, worthless wretch. Then God reminds me that there were some other people who also fell short.

We have talked about Abraham's faith when he told a half truth twice, and he passed his wife off as his sister because he was afraid that he would be killed. That is not much of a spiritual giant to me. The Bible says that he stumbled not at the promise of God that Isaac would be born, yet they gave up on God by having Ishmael and producing the nation that is constantly tormenting Israel today. It says in Romans that God calls those things that were not as though they were because he saw the end of Abraham's life, who he would be, and who he would become. God looks down on you and me and says, "I am the author and the finisher of your faith. He that began a good work in you is able to bring it to completion." He has called those things in our life that were not as though they were. He calls us to come home faithful and good servant. What a God we have. What mercy and grace and what love. How can we not love him when he is so powerful?

# DEMONIC AFFLICTIONS

The next illness that we are going to explore is demonic afflictions, which are illness that are caused by demonic powers and spirits. Not all illness is caused by demonic spirits, and not all demonic spirits cause illness. There can be demon possession without disease. There can be illnesses that are not related to demonic spirits. What we will learn, as we look at the scriptures, is that some demonic spirits cause disease and affliction.

Mark 9:17–19 says:

> And one of the multitude answered and said, Master, I have brought unto thee my son, which hath a dumb spirit; and wheresoever he taketh him, he teareth him; and he foameth, and gnasheth with his teeth, and pineth away: and I spake to thy disciples that they should cast him out; and they could not. He answereth him, and saith, O faithless generation, how long shall I be with you? how long shall I suffer you? bring him unto me.

I often wonder if Jesus Christ might ask us today how long he needs to be with us and how long he must suffer us because of our unbelief that we cannot do the work that he asks us to do. We would be capable of doing these works if we would just believe God and be obedient to his Spirit. He rebuked his disciples when he said unto them, "Oh faithless generation." Where is our faith and our commitment to God?

Mark 9:20–24 says:

And they brought him unto him: and when he saw him, straightway the spirit tare him; and he fell on the ground, and wallowed foaming. And he asked his father, How long is it ago since this came unto him? And he said, Of a child. And ofttimes it hath cast him into the fire, and into the waters, to destroy him: but if thou canst do any thing, have compassion on us, and help us. Jesus said unto him, If thou canst believe, all things are possible to him that believeth. And straightway the father of the child cried out, and said with tears, Lord, I believe; help thou mine unbelief.

I think that sometimes we find ourselves in the same situation as this father in the way that we have a little bit of faith and a little bit of belief. We know in our hearts that God can do anything and all things that he says he can do, but our big problem is that our flesh gets in the way. We just cannot quite believe, so we must cry out as this man did, saying that we do believe, but please help our unbelief.

Mark 9:25–29 says:

When Jesus saw that the people came running together, he rebuked the foul spirit, saying unto him, Thou dumb and deaf spirit, I charge thee, come out of him, and enter no more into him. And the spirit cried, and rent him sore, and came out of him: and he was as one dead; insomuch that many said, He is dead. But Jesus took him by the hand, and lifted him up; and he arose. And when he was come into the house, his disciples asked him privately, Why could not we cast him out? And he said unto them, This kind can come forth by nothing, but by prayer and fasting.

In the passages above, we learn that the man's son had epilepsy, which was caused by a demonic spirit. Jesus cast out the demonic spirit, and the child was healed.

I would like to share a couple of testimonies with you that relate to the passage above. One of them that we are going to come back to is the deaf and dumb spirit. The first one that I would like to share happened when I first got saved and filled with the Spirit. At this time, I started working with four young men who were called into the ministry. We started out with a Bible study, and after a while, they said to me, "We want more than just a Bible study. We want to take what we are learning and put it to use."

Of course, as a young man with a lack of knowledge and wisdom, I often opened my mouth and inserted my foot. So I said, "Where is the greatest need in Dallas?"

"Fed Mart parking lot," they said.

Then I told them of how a man named David Wilkerson got someone to play the trumpet, which drew a crowd, and then he preached to the crowd. I then said to them, "Next Friday night, one of you young men can play your trombone, the other one can play his guitar, and we'll go out to the Fed Mart parking lot and preach."

The next Friday night, they came at about 9:30, which is when people would begin to gather. We drove to Fed Mart, parked the car, and sat on the hood of the car. Now I must tell you that we were the weird ones out there; we were the strange ones. There were all kinds of things going on out there. We saw twelve- year-old kids walking around with bottles of whiskey because their parents handed then twenty bucks and said, "Do whatever you want, but just don't come home till after midnight because we don't want you here." It went from this age all the way up to people in their late teens and early twenties who were drinking, doing drugs, and generally causing all kinds of problems. This went to the extreme of some even having sex in the backs of pick-ups. It was a rough, rowdy crowd.

We sat there for a while. Nobody came over to us and nothing happened. I turned to the young man with the trombone and said, "Why don't you play 'When the Saints Come Marching In, and we'll start marching up and down the parking lot until we get a crowd?" That kid was so petrified that he could not play a note.

One of the other young men with us who had been delivered from drugs and was a wild kind of character said, "Give me the trombone." He could make noise but could not play a song. Nevertheless, we started marching all the way down the length of the parking lot with everyone looking at us like we were weirdoes, and when we got near the end, a young man came up to us and said, "What are you guys doing out here?"

I said, "Follow us, and I will tell you."

He said, "No way. I am not going with you guys."

We went on to the end of the parking lot, and we still had not drawn a crowd, so we turned and went back. As we were heading back, again a young man came up to us and said, "What are you guys doing here?"

Then the young man with the guitar, who had written his testimony in a song, was anointed with the Holy Spirit at that moment and said, "I'm going to tell you." He then began to sing his testimony in song. After he finished singing, the young man who had been delivered from drugs gave his testimony. Then I proclaimed, in a preaching way, the plan of salvation.

When I finished preaching, I said, "I am going to pray." So I bowed my head to pray that those who were lost would come to Christ, and when I stopped praying, I looked up and saw this young man standing in front of me.

He said to me, "This Jesus that you are talking about, can he forgive me?" I said, "Yes, he can forgive you."

He then said, "You do not understand. All of the alcohol that I have been drinking and all of the girls that I have slept with, can he forgive me for that?" I said, "Yes. He can."

He then said to me, "You still do not understand. I was a drug addict, and I fried my brain on drugs. I can no longer concentrate, think, and do the things that a person is supposed to do. Can he forgive that?"

I said, "Yes. He can."

"I wish I could understand it. If only my mind was clear enough," he responded.

I did not know what to do, so I said, "I am going to pray for you, if you would like me to."

He said, "I would like that."

I told him that I was going to ask God to clear up his mind so that he could understand salvation. I then reached over and put my hand on him and said, "In the name of Jesus Christ, I ask that the Holy Spirit come and touch your mind and clear it up so that you might think clearly and that you might come to a saving knowledge of Jesus Christ."

This young man then started jumping up and down, screaming and yelling, at which point I got embarrassed and wanted to go hide. He then said to me, "Man oh man. I can think. I can reason. I can concentrate for the first time that I can remember in my life. God has just healed me." He then accepted Christ. Also there were two young girls who had accepted Christ.

The next Sunday morning, they came to Sunday school and church with the other young people. After they had been coming to the other Bible study that I taught on Tuesday nights, one of the girls came to me and said, "I have a nephew who is fourteen months of age. The doctors have diagnosed him with epilepsy, and he is not responding to the medication."

The Lord then spoke to me, bringing me to Mark chapter 9, and said, "This boy has a demonic spirit, and you need to pray for him." I then asked the young lady if she would bring her nephew over. I told her what the Lord had said to her and read to her from the scripture.

A few days later, she brought the child over to me. As I approached the child, he would start screaming. Finally, I just laid my hand on him and said, "In the name of Jesus Christ, I command that this spirit and all of the demonic spirits in him come out in Jesus' name." Later I found out that the doctors claimed they had misdiagnosed him because he never had another seizure. They could not find a single thing wrong with the child, and he was set free from the seizures.

God had miraculously touched this young child through deliverance, and the demonic spirit had come out of him.

One evening, in our home, I was teaching a Bible study to a group of drug addicts. This evening, there was a young woman present who was a prostitute. She came to me and said, "I want to receive Christ as my Savior."

As I started to minister to her, she suddenly became totally deaf and dumb. She could not speak, hear, nor understand. The Spirit of God then said to me, "She has a spirit of deaf and dumbness, and you need to bind that spirit." Notice that he did not say to cast it out because if you cast out a spirit from a house that is not filled with

Christ, that spirit will go out and find seven demons worse than itself and come back to inhabit that clean house. So what I needed to do was bind the spirits so that they could no longer have an effect on her and then show her the gospel.

Once she realized that she needed Christ and that she was demon-possessed, she could then be delivered and receive Jesus Christ. At that point, the house would then be clean and filled with the Holy Spirit. I laid my hand on her and bound the spirits in the name of Jesus, then shared with her the gospel. She realized that she needed to be saved and delivered, she prayed and received Christ, then the spirits were cast out, and she was free.

Luke 13:10–17 says:

> And he was teaching in one of the synagogues on the sabbath. And, behold, there was a woman which had a spirit of infirmity eighteen years, and was bowed together, and could in no wise lift up herself. And when Jesus saw her, he called her to him, and said unto her, Woman, thou art loosed from thine infirmity. And he laid his hands on her: and immediately she was made straight, and glorified God. And the ruler of the synagogue answered with indignation, because that Jesus had healed on the sabbath day, and said unto the people, There are six days in which men ought to work: in them therefore come and be healed, and not on the sabbath day. The Lord then answered him, and said, Thou hypocrite, doth not each one of you on the sabbath loose his ox or his ass from the stall, and lead him away to watering? And ought not this woman, being a daughter of Abraham, whom Satan hath bound, lo, these eighteen years, be loosed from this bond on the sabbath day? And when he had said these things, all his adversaries were ashamed: and all the people rejoiced for all the glorious things that were done by him.

Once again, we see the Lord healing on the Sabbath day. He did this to show the Pharisees that their law was legalistic and rigid and that it had no place for love. He wanted them to understand that God came to love, to set free, and to deliver, not only spiritually but also physically. He said, "I was wounded for your transgressions. I was bruised for your iniquities, and by my stripes you were healed." He bore the stripes that we might be healed.

# ABUSING OUR BODIES

nother affliction that we are going to learn about is the abusing of our bodies. I think that this is one area where we are guiltier than we may realize. We, because of overworking and trying to take on more than we can handle, are many times in a state of sleep deprivation. This can lead to all kinds of problems, including illnesses which affect one mentally, physically, emotionally, and spiritually.

Philippians 2:25–30 says:

> Yet I supposed it necessary to send to you Epaphroditus, my brother, and companion in labor, and fellow soldier, but your messenger, and he that ministered to my wants. For he longed after you all, and was full of heaviness, because that ye had heard that he had been sick. For indeed he was sick nigh unto death: but God had mercy on him; and not on him only, but on me also, lest I should have sorrow upon sorrow. I sent him therefore the more carefully, that, when ye see him again, ye may rejoice, and that I may be the less sorrowful. Receive him therefore in the Lord with all gladness; and hold such in reputation: because for the work of Christ he was nigh unto death, not regarding his life, to supply your lack of service toward me.

The passages above make it clear that Epaphroditus, in overworking, had brought upon himself a sickness and an illness that almost killed him. He worked until he had become worn-out, resulting in a condition in which he almost died.

I once knew a missionary who would push himself for twenty hours per day for days at a time. After doing this for several months, he became exhausted. Due to sleep deprivation, he had a nervous breakdown. It took him months to be healed, but God was gracious and healed him. Most of us try to do too much because we think that if we do not, we have failed man and God. The missionary was a missionary in India. He refused to come home on furlough, worked twenty-hour days trying to minister to the needs of the Indian people, and finally ended up with great problems due to his sleep deprivation. This type of abuse is often referred to as burning out. It appears to be productive but is out of God's will because it is usually done in the flesh and not led by the Spirit.

There is another type of abuse which is much more self-centered and more destructive because this abuse will also destroy the spirit.

First Corinthians 6:9 says:

> Know ye not that the unrighteous shall not inherit the kingdom of God? Be not deceived: neither fornicators, nor idolaters, nor adulterers, nor effeminate, nor abusers of themselves with mankind.

Romans 1:21–32 says:

> Because that, when they knew God, they glorified him not as God, neither were thankful; but became vain in their imaginations, and their foolish heart was darkened. Professing themselves to be wise, they became fools, And changed the glory of the uncorruptible God into an image made like to corruptible man, and to birds, and fourfooted beasts, and creeping things. Wherefore God also gave them up to uncleanness through the lusts of their own hearts, to dishonour their own bodies between themselves: Who changed the truth of God into a lie, and worshipped and served the creature more than the Creator, who is blessed for ever. Amen. For this cause God gave them up unto vile affections: for even their women did change the natural use into that which is against nature: And likewise also the men, leaving

the natural use of the woman, burned in their lust one toward another; men with men working that which is unseemly, and receiving in themselves that recompence of their error which was meet. And even as they did not like to retain God in their knowledge, God gave them over to a reprobate mind, to do those things which are not convenient; Being filled with all unrighteousness, fornication, wickedness, covetousness, maliciousness; full of envy, murder, debate, deceit, malignity; whisperers, Backbiters, haters of God, despiteful, proud, boasters, inventors of evil things, disobedient to parents, Without understanding, covenantbreakers, without natural affection, implacable, unmerciful: Who knowing the judgment of God, that they which commit such things are worthy of death, not only do the same, but have pleasure in them that do them.

These passages deal specifically with homosexuality and the consequences of this self-gratification.

Proverbs 5:1–13 says:

My son, attend unto my wisdom, and bow thine ear to my understanding: That thou mayest regard discretion, and that thy lips may keep knowledge. For the lips of a strange woman drop as an honeycomb, and her mouth is smoother than oil: But her end is bitter as wormwood, sharp as a two-edged sword. Her feet go down to death; her steps take hold on hell. Lest thou shouldest ponder the path of life, her ways are moveable, that thou canst not know them. Hear me now therefore, O ye children, and depart not from the words of my mouth. Remove thy way far from her, and come not nigh the door of her house: Lest thou give thine honour unto others, and thy years unto the cruel: Lest strangers be filled with thy wealth; and thy labours be in the house of a stranger; And thou mourn at the last, when thy flesh and thy body are consumed, And say, How have I hated instruction, and my heart despised reproof; And have not obeyed the voice of my teachers, nor inclined mine ear to them that instructed me!

Proverbs 7:1–23 says:

My son, keep my words, And treasure my commands within you. Keep my commands and live, And my law as the apple of your eye. Bind them on your fingers; Write them on the tablet of your heart. Say to wisdom, "You *are* my sister," And call understanding *your* nearest kin, That they may keep you from the immoral woman, From the seductress *who* flatters with her words. For at the window of my house I looked through my lattice, And saw among the simple, I perceived among the youths, A young man devoid of understanding, Passing along the street near her corner; And he took the path to her house In the twilight, in the evening, In the black and dark night. And there a woman met him, *With* the attire of a harlot, and a crafty heart. She *was* loud and rebellious, Her feet would not stay at home. At times *she was* outside, at times in the open square, Lurking at every corner. So she caught him and kissed him; With an impudent face she said to him: "*I have* peace offerings with me; Today I have paid my vows. So I came out to meet you, Diligently to seek your face, And I have found you. I have spread my bed with tapestry, Colored coverings of Egyptian linen. I have perfumed my bed With myrrh, aloes, and cinnamon. Come, let us take our fill of love until morning; Let us delight ourselves with love. For my husband *is* not at home; He has gone on a long journey; He has taken a bag of money with him, *And* will come home on the appointed day." With her enticing speech she caused him to yield, With her flattering lips she seduced him. Immediately he went after her, as an ox goes to the slaughter, Or as a fool to the correction of the stocks,[fn] Till an arrow struck his liver. As a bird hastens to the snare, He did not know it *would cost* his life.

Proverbs 23:26–35 says:

My son, give me your heart, And let your eyes observe my ways. For a harlot *is* a deep pit, And a seductress *is* a narrow well. She also lies in wait as *for* a victim, And increases the unfaithful among men. Who has woe? Who has sorrow? Who has contentions? Who has complaints? Who has wounds without cause? Who has redness of eyes? Those who linger long at the wine, Those who go in search of mixed wine. Do not look on the wine when it is red, When it sparkles in the cup, *When* it swirls around smoothly; At the last it bites like a serpent, And stings like a viper. Your eyes will see strange things, And your heart will utter perverse things. Yes, you will be like one who lies down in the midst of the sea, Or like one who lies at the top of the mast, *saying:* "They have struck me, *but* I was not hurt; They have beaten me, but I did not feel *it.* When shall I awake, that I may seek another *drink?*"

The results of adultery or fornication, more specifically with a prostitute, may result in physical death caused by sexually transmitted diseases.

# MOLDING OF THE SPIRIT

The next illness that we are going to learn about is the molding of the spirit. In other words, it is when God uses an illness as a molding of the spirit. There are two kinds of chastisement described in the scriptures. One, which we already learned about, is when you are being spanked for sin. The other, which is described in Hebrews, is a molding chastisement, and it may involve illness. It is a molding type of chastisement when God is trying to mold our spirits into the realm that he wants us to be.

An illustration of this, which may help us to understand it better, starts by saying that before we get saved, everything we do is in the flesh. Then, with salvation, our spirit is born. Finally, with death, the flesh dies, and one becomes a totally spiritual being. The spirit works against the flesh, and the flesh works against the spirit. When something comes against us, we react in the flesh.

Jesus had much trouble with his disciples in trying to get them out of the flesh and into the spirit. We can look at the Lord's prayer in two different ways, either totally spiritual or totally fleshly. I really think that it has a double meaning. For example, "Give unto us this day our daily bread." The bread represents both the flesh and the spirit of our Lord. If you go through the Lord's prayer and ask him to show it to you in a completely spiritual sense, you will be amazed at how it totally opens to you. The molding of the spirit is where God allows things to happen to our flesh so that we quit reacting in the flesh and start reacting in the spirit.

A good example would be if someone were to come up and do something wrong to you. The flesh wants to get even or more than get even; however, the spirit says that we must forgive and pray for those who despitefully use us. If we begin to react in the spirit, then an inner peace, an inner joy, and an inner fullness develops. Then we start walking like Jesus, who hung on the cross and said, "Father, forgive them. They do not know what they're doing." This is what we are talking about in relation to the molding of the spirit.

The word *chastise*, as used in Hebrews 12, means to refine or to make purer in style. This is not always a physical affliction but can be. Job, at first, lost all his possessions, and then he was afflicted physically. Job 1:6–7 says:

> Now there was a day when the sons of God came to present themselves before the Lord, and Satan came also among them. And the Lord said unto Satan, Whence comest thou? Then Satan answered the Lord, and said, From going to and fro in the earth, and from walking up and down in it.

Have you ever thought about the fact that Satan has free access to the throne of God? He does, and he stands at the throne, accusing God and accusing you and me. God has established certain rules and regulations that he will and must follow. Satan is standing before God, accusing him of not following the rules and of showing favoritism. God told Satan that it was the prayer of saints who gave him the right to do certain things. Therefore, God said, in Ezekiel, "I searched through the entire world looking for a man who could intercede, and I could not find one." I think that sometimes we fail to realize how important prayer is, especially intercessory prayer.

I read a case where a missionary who was in Africa amongst a violent, cannibalistic tribe was driving one night when his car broke down. These cannibals were there, looking to see who they could kill and take back to eat. In the main church where the missionary had come out of, there was a deacon who was awakened by the Lord that night. God laid on his heart the urgency to pray for the missionary couple. He called the twelve other deacons at the church and told them that it was imperative that they get to the church and intercede. They stayed there all night, praying.

When the next day came around, they all went home with the feeling that everything was fine, even though they had no idea of what had happened. The missionary couple, whose car broke down, got up the next day, went for help, and everything was fine. Several weeks later, the head of the cannibalistic tribe, along with some tribe members, came into one of their revival meetings and accepted Christ. Afterward, he came up to them and said, "I must tell you people something. The reason why I am here and why I accepted Christ tonight was that several weeks ago, we came upon the car with the missionary who is speaking here tonight. As we got ready to approach the car, which had nobody around it, thirteen men suddenly came around the car with spears and stood there all night. Those men were not there when we started going toward the car but suddenly appeared."

He then described the features of some of these men, and they were the exact features of the deacons who were praying for the missionary. He then said, "We realize that our god was the wrong god and that his God is the real God. This is the reason we came tonight."

It is immensely powerful when you start realizing the strength and the power of God, especially when you go into true intercessory prayer. Job 1:8–12 says:

> And the Lord said unto Satan, Hast thou considered my servant Job, that there is none like him in the earth, a perfect and an upright man, one that feareth God, and escheweth evil? Then Satan answered the Lord, and said, Doth Job fear God for nought? Hast not thou made a hedge about him, and about his house, and about all that he hath on every side? thou hast blessed the work of his hands, and his substance is increased in the land. But put forth thine hand now, and touch all that he hath, and he will curse thee to thy face. And the Lord said unto Satan, Behold, all that he hath is in thy power; only upon himself put not forth thine hand. So Satan went forth from the presence of the Lord.

When we read the book of Job, we come to realize that there is not one thing that can happen to us unless God allows it. This is the sovereignty of God.

Job 2:1–3 says:

> Again there was a day when the sons of God came to present themselves before the Lord, and Satan came also among them to present himself before the Lord. And the Lord said unto Satan, From whence comest thou? And Satan answered the Lord, and said, From going to and fro in the earth, and from walking up and down in it. And the Lord said unto Satan, Hast thou considered my servant Job, that there is none like him in the earth, a perfect and an upright man, one that feareth God, and escheweth evil? and still he holdeth fast his integrity, although thou movedst me against him, to destroy him without cause.

If we read the book of Job, we will find out that when Job started on his journey, he said, "I have heard of thee by the hearing of the ear: but now mine eye seeth thee." Job knew about God, but now he *knows* him. He also said, "The thing that I feared came upon me." There are certain things that happen in our life that are strange in this way.

There is one thing that I feared and never wanted to happen to me. I spoke of it when I told the story about the man who severed his spinal cord and had the halo screwed into his skull. The halo screwed into my skull is what I am speaking about; it just gives me the creeps! I have always said that I never ever want that to happen to me. Well, several years ago, I had to have five hours of neck surgery, and they screwed that steel halo to my head. The good thing about it was that I was under anesthetic when they did it and that they had taken it off before I woke up. I did not know it until I felt the holes in my head and touched the blood that was dripping out of them. When I realized it, I asked the doctor, "What's this?"

He said, "We put a halo on you. I told you that we were going to do it." "No, you did not," I said to him.

"Did I forget to tell you?" he said.

"Yeah," I answered. This is just like when Job said the things that he feared came upon him. Molding Job is what God is really doing here. He is molding him into the image of his Son, Jesus Christ. Every one of us, if we are truly saved, have said to God at some time, "God, I want to be just like Jesus." We may not have known what we prayed because God says, "I want you to be like my Son more than you'll ever want to be, but are you willing to let me make you like him?"

We, as Christians, love the gospel right up until it talks about the gospel of suffering. Jesus learned obedience through suffering, even until his death on the cross. Some may say, "No, no, no. That is not part of the gospel. If you get saved, there will not be any more suffering. You won't have any more pain."

"You haven't read the Bible," I say to them. When we get to heaven, the least of our concerns will be what we suffered for Christ. When we get to heaven, we are not going to thank God for the healings, blessings, and all the good things. We are going to thank him for all the hard times that molded us into the image of Jesus Christ. Those hard times are what purify our faith and will eventually bring us into his presence with an abundant entrance. This is where Job is.

"Naked came I out of my mother's womb and naked shall I return thither." His wife said, "Curse God and die."

Job trusted God. However, Job did have some hang-ups. He needed for God to do a work in his life. Yet God said, "There's not a man better than Job." None of us are like Christ; no matter where we arrive, we still have another step to go.

Paul said, "I rejoice in the afflictions and persecution, because in my weakness I can put on His strength." Job 2:4-6 says:

> And Satan answered the Lord, and said, Skin for skin, yea, all that a man hath will he give for his life. But put forth thine hand now, and touch his bone and his flesh, and he will curse thee to thy face. And the Lord said unto Satan, Behold, he is in thine hand; but save his life.

Job's biggest complaint was that he wanted to die. He had a sense and a knowing that God was not going to let him die, but he was going to have to suffer until he found the deliverance. Aren't we the same way? When we get sick or have something bad happen, we say, "Oh God, I wish I could die. Oh Jesus, just hurry up and come." When everything is moving along well, we say, "Lord, just hold off on me a little while. I have got a friend who needs to be saved." God help us that we may arrive at the place where he wants for us to be.

Job 2:9–10 says:

> Then said his wife unto him, Dost thou still retain thine integrity? curse God, and die. But he said unto her, Thou speakest as one of the foolish women speaketh. What? shall we receive good at the hand of God, and shall we not receive evil? In all this did not Job sin with his lips.

Job 19:25–27 says:

> For I know that my Redeemer liveth, and that he shall stand at the latter day upon the earth: and though after my skin worms destroy this body, yet in my flesh shall I see God: whom I shall see for myself, and mine eyes shall behold, and not another; though my reins be consumed within me.

Before this point, Job may not have been certain that his redeemer was alive; now he is sure of it. As we come to this point, we can really see what God is doing.

There was a time in my life when some things happened, and I reached the point where I could not pray; I did not have any faith left. I felt like Paul when he said that he was pressed out of measure and he had the sentence of death in him. There was simply nothing left. I was physically, mentally, and spiritually bankrupt. I just had to say to the Lord, "You know what the situation is, and all I can do is just trust you. There is no use in praying because you already know what I want and need out of this situation. All I can do is just trust you."

Do you know what God wanted me to learn? That God is God! I do not know how to tell anyone this. The Holy Spirit will just have to show it to them. When you have come to the point where you know that God is God, then you will know what I am talking about. It brings you to the point of stripping you of all your strengths, and the only thing you can do is trust in God.

Don't we all at times feel a little spiritual? Sometimes I feel really spiritual, where spiritual pride is just reeking out of me, and like I have all the answers. Just like Job's friends, they had his answers, but they were so far off that it was pathetic. Paul was so powerful as a witness and servant of God because he was so broken. Paul, as a Pharisee, should have known the scriptures and recognized Christ. Instead he persecuted Christians and stood by when Stephen was ordered to be stoned to death. Paul said, "Who am I to judge any man? I am the chief amongst sinners."

When God strips us of everything, we arrive at the point at which all we can do is look up. All we have left is his faith. When this happens, we come to realize that we do not need a mountain of faith but that just a mustard seed is enough. When we come to that "mustard seed" of faith, we find that we have a big enough God and that he can do anything.

I would like to share something that is totally contrary to anything that you have ever been taught but that is the truth. You may not believe it now, but someday you will. We do not need much faith; we just need a bigger God. A little faith in a big God is a whole lot better than a lot of faith in a mediocre God. It is when we find out how big our God is that we realize how blessed that we are. We do not have to have a lot of faith, just a little bit. How many times in the scripture did Jesus say, "If you can believe, all things are possible" and then people say, "Lord, I believe, but help thou my unbelief"? This is where we are. We need to become spiritual beings who can totally trust him and walk with him.

Job 23:10 says:

> But he knoweth the way that I take: when he hath tried me, I shall come forth as gold.

First Peter 1:3–7 says:

> Blessed be the God and Father of our Lord Jesus Christ, which according to his abundant mercy hath begotten us again unto a lively hope by the resurrection of Jesus Christ from the dead, to an inheritance incorruptible, and undefiled, and that fadeth not away, reserved in heaven for you, who are kept by the power of God through faith unto salvation ready to be revealed in the last time. Wherein ye greatly rejoice, though

now for a season, if need be, ye are in heaviness through manifold temptations: that the trial of your faith, being much more precious than of gold that perisheth, though it be tried with fire, might be found unto praise and honor and glory at the appearing of Jesus Christ.

If we were to look at the above passage and read it backward, we would be in a great trial. We would be in a great trial because we need it. This is God's love. He says, "You need this trial, which is only going to be for a season, so hang in there."

Have you ever stopped and thought about the saying, "And this too will pass"? Also, in the above, he is saying that our faith needs to be purified and needs to be tried.

There is a parable that illustrates a person continuously badgering for something that they want, and finally, to get rid of this person, the badgered one says, "I am going to just give it to him." Many preachers advocate that this is what we are supposed to do; I think not. If we keep badgering God long enough, then he will give it to us. It is just like with some parents; if their kids badger them long enough, they just give in. They know it is not good for them, but they finally give in because they get tired of listening to it. This is like saying, "Okay, you're going to learn your lesson by getting what you should not have." This happened to the Israelites when they lusted after meat in the wilderness.

Numbers 11:18–20 says:

> Then you shall say to the people, "Consecrate yourselves for tomorrow, and you shall eat meat; for you have wept in the hearing of the Lord, saying, 'Who will give us meat to eat? For *it was* well with us in Egypt.' Therefore the Lord will give you meat, and you shall eat. "You shall eat, not one day, nor two days, nor five days, nor ten days, nor twenty days, but *for* a whole month, until it comes out of your nostrils and becomes loathsome to you, because you have despised the Lord who is among you, and have wept before Him, saying, "Why did we ever come up out of Egypt?'"

There is so much teaching on prayer today that is wrong because the scripture is taken out of context; they are not reading what he is saying. He did not say that this is the thing to do; however, there are people who believe that you just keep pounding on him until he gives you what you want. He said, "You have not because you ask amiss after your own lust and your own desires, and not with God's will."

Sometimes God will say to us, "You need to have this in your life so that it will change your life."

Paul said, "Lord, take this thorn from me." Three times he asked God for this, and three times God said no.

Finally God said, "My grace is sufficient for you. In your weakness you will be strong."

Paul said that it was given to him so he would not exalt himself above measure. Sometimes God may give us a thorn in the flesh because we're going through a time when spiritual pride is entering in or when other things are happening and he feels that we need something to buffet us until we can learn to walk in humbleness.

Job 23:12–14 says:

> My foot hath held his steps, his way have I kept, and not declined. Neither have I gone back from the commandment of his lips; I have esteemed the words of his mouth more than my necessary food. But he is in one mind, and who can turn him? And what his soul desireth, even that he doeth. For he performeth the thing that is appointed for me: and many such things are with him.

Job came to understand that he could not die and that God allowed this to happen to give him the opportunity to do something in his life that would mold him into the image of Christ.

When we are in the midst of our own life's trials, and everything seems to be going the wrong way, we are so busy complaining to God about how miserable we feel that we aren't listening to what he is trying to tell us. When we can finally get through all the "garbage" that we present to him, we can finally say,

"God, this is not going to go away unless you take it away. Maybe I should open my spiritual ears and eyes to see and hear what you are trying to do in my life."

Job went in and out of this. He cursed the day that he was born, and then he would find insight. Then he would say, "I wish I could die" and then find insight once again. He went back and forth with this. This is a picture of what can happen in our life if we could just listen and see what God is trying to do. With all the illnesses that can happen to us, this is probably the one that does us the most good because it is the one that makes us into the image of Jesus Christ. This is also the toughest and hardest one.

Job 42:5 says:

> I have heard of thee by the hearing of the ear; but now mine eye seeth thee.

God brought Job to his revelation by asking him, "Job, where were you when I created the world?" He was telling Job to open his eyes and look around because he knew that Job could not help but see it.

At one time in my life, I was an atheist. I looked around and saw the hypocrisy of those who called themselves Christians. Knowing the Bible and realizing that I was far from where I needed to be, I decided to reject it all together. Then, when I had to take a comparative zoology course, I realized the number or holes in my atheistic life's theory. God deals with this type of thing in Jeremiah. The Bible says that from a piece of wood, one burns a part of it to cook a meal; makes other things out of part of it; and then, out of another part, makes an idol to bow down and worship to. One can take that idol anywhere but must carry it everywhere because it has no legs or arms that are able to make itself move. It cannot hear you or speak to you, but you still bow down to worship it. Your mind has gone so far that it cannot even reason.

When we reject God, this is what happens to our mind. The Bible says that the foolish reject the things of God. The most miraculous thing that absolutely fascinates me is that you can take an ovum, put a sperm into it, and create one little cell which will ultimately grow into a person who can think and reason. If we stop and think about this, then we realize that there must be a God. It boggles my mind to think that this cell can grow into such a complex person and each one be so vastly different.

Job came to know that he served a living Savior that he would see. Job also came to understand that he was being tried by a God who was able to see him through the trial and purify his faith as gold. By far, the greatest thing that happened to Job was that he now saw the living God; God had become alive.

# MINISTERING LIKE JESUS

S o far we have seen some of the means and ways by which Jesus Christ ministered. We have seen some of the ways that the Old Testament prophets ministered and how God used them in healing. We have seen how the apostles were used, and I have shared a few of my personal testimonies. I would like to conclude our study by looking at how Jesus Christ ministered. I feel that it is important for us to walk in the way that he walked, which is what I hope for us to accomplish in this final lesson.

Something that is especially important to keep in mind is that Jesus did not perform any recorded miracles until he was baptized and received the Holy Spirit. Afterward, he then set out to do the work of the heavenly Father. There is one thing that is very vital and important that we are going to see, and that is the whole central theme of Jesus's life and ministry. That is the thing he said over and over, "I do no works of my own and I speak no words that are my own."

If we stop and think about this, we cannot help but ask ourselves, "What kind of problems are we in today?" Ninety-nine percent of our words are probably our own, and if we are lucky, 1 percent may be the Lord's.

Jesus made the statement, "I do not speak any words unless they are my Father's words, and I don't do any works unless they are my Father's works." In contrast, we go about our way, doing all of the things that we want to do, and then if it does not work, we go to the Lord to see if there's something else that we should have been doing. Jesus did not do it that way; his whole life and being was committed to doing his Father's works. He did this not to receive any glory upon himself but only desired to glorify his Father. He knew by doing this that his Father would then glorify him afterward. Jesus tells us that if we do the works of the Father, we will glorify the Son who will then in turn glorify us, not for our glory but for his glory. This is what we need to strive for.

Isaiah 11:1–3 says:

> And there shall come forth a rod out of the stem of Jesse, and a Branch shall grow out of his roots: and the Spirit of the Lord shall rest upon him, the spirit of wisdom and understanding, the spirit of counsel and might, the spirit of knowledge and of the fear of the Lord; and shall make him of quick understanding in the fear of the Lord. And he shall not judge after the sight of his eyes, neither reprove after the hearing of his ears.

Notice all the things that are going to rest upon him: the spirit of understanding, the spirit of counsel and might, the spirit of knowledge, and the spirit of the fear of the Lord. Notice what it says next: "And shall make Him of quick understanding in the fear of the Lord." It seems kind of strange that Jesus Christ is going to understand the fear of the Lord and that it is going to make him of quick understanding in the fear of the Lord. If we stop and think about this for a few minutes and reflect on what Proverbs says, it tells us that the fear of the Lord is the hatred of sin.

In knowing this, let us now turn this around to make it where we can really understand it. If we do not hate sin, then we do not fear God. This makes it truly clear, doesn't it? In other words, if we do not hate sin, then we do not fear the judgment of God. Therefore the scripture says that he will make Jesus Christ of quick understanding in the fear of God. This is important because Jesus took on the flesh of man, which is not clean and pure. The flesh of man is first driven by survival, isn't it? For example, if a child is hungry, what does the child do? The child cries. What happens then? Mom feeds the child. Therefore the child is taught the lesson that if it is hungry, then all it must do is cry. If the child wants something else, then it cries, too, and Mom comes running. It does not take a child long to learn this.

God said that his Son was going to get a quick understanding in the fear of the Lord. In other words, he is going to put his flesh under subjection to the Spirit very quickly; otherwise, he is not going to live the perfect life that is necessary for redemption. Remember that earlier we talked about there being two ways to get to heaven. And that if there were not two ways, then we would not have salvation. When Jesus Christ died and took the sins of the world upon him, the only way that God could resurrect him was that he had not sinned. This is a way to heaven, living a perfect life.

I am sorry, but there are not any of us who are going to make it that way. The only one who did, we crucified, and he took all our sins upon him. It is essential that we understand there are two ways to get to heaven. Knowing this, we can now begin to understand why the Spirit made Jesus Christ of quick understanding in the fear of the Lord and the consequences of sin. Because death was the wages of sin, if he sinned, there would be no one to redeem him, and the world would all die. This is what Jesus wants us to understand; however, it seems to be so difficult for us because we do not immediately see the consequences from God for sin. We may feel guilty, but after a while, we become guilty of so much that we think, "Oh well, what is another sin?"

The Lord says that we must not walk by sight but be led by the Spirit. What he is trying to get us to see and understand is that we must become Spirit-led people, Spirit-guided people, Spirit-trusting people, and Spirit-walking people. If everything else fails, then we will turn to the Spirit. We want to do it in our own effort with our own compassion first.

This is the same place where we get into trouble, is it not? We think, "Hey, I am a sinner, so I better cut you some slack. I'm not perfect, so who am I to require that you be perfect." It is not I who requires that we live this life. It is the Word. Regardless of where I am, I cannot excuse your sins nor can you excuse mine. If we could understand this, then we would help people greatly. If we excuse and make excuses for sins, it will not bring peace, victory, or joy.

David, when he was broken and in agony because of his sin, said unto the Lord, "Restore unto me the joy of thy salvation." The only way that we can have the joy of God's salvation is to repent of our sins and be washed in the blood. Then we can have fellowship with him again. If I regard iniquity in my heart, the Lord shall not hear me. Yet we excuse sin and justify sin in our brothers and sisters because we are sinners and cannot sit in judgment. This is keeping them from the victory, power, peace, and joy that God has for them.

Understanding this, we must instead confront them in their sins. If you are asking yourself, "How can I?" look at the apostle Paul; he did not waste any words. One might say, "But he was more righteous than I am." He may have been, but he also said that he was chief among sinners.

Two things that I had to learn as a pastor was that God honors the office and never the man. When I stood in the office, I was the spokesperson for God. It does not make any difference what an individual's life is like. One cannot excuse sins because the pastor has sinned or because the teacher has sinned. You must answer to God for what the Word and the Holy Spirit says to you. God has chosen imperfect men to hold his office as teachers, preachers, and pastors. He is using them to motivate and move people in the right way.

In Isaiah 11:3, the Bible says that the Son of God shall not judge after the sight of his eyes and neither reprove after the hearing of his ears. He said this because he was in a fleshy body and knew its weaknesses and desires. If he slipped into the flesh, he would no longer do the works of his Father, so he had to guard against it; we do also. We must be bold, be blunt, and do what the Spirit tells us. If the Spirit is leading, then I do not care how bold we may be. People will receive it because they want the truth. The truth will set us free; excuses keep us in bondage. Justification does not give us victory, but the truth does.

Isaiah 11:4–5 says:

> But with righteousness shall he judge the poor, and reprove with equity for the meek of the earth: and he shall smite the earth with the rod of his mouth, and with the breath of his lips shall he slay the wicked. And righteousness shall be the girdle of his loins, and faithfulness the girdle of his reins.

When Jesus was born, God took on a totally new dimension, which was that of the flesh of man. Jesus now had to deal with the effects of the flesh, such as emotional sensitivity to one's fleshly feelings. Jesus, who was and is God, is now housed in a fleshly tabernacle and does not have the freedom of the Spirit. Jesus was housed in the same flesh as you and I. He had all the same biological functions, such as getting tired, becoming hungry, and all our other emotions. He had to learn to put the flesh under the subjection of the Spirit.

In Hebrews 5:8, the Word says that he learned obedience through suffering. Jesus put himself under the authority of his Father to do his will rather than what he would desire from his fleshly emotions and understanding. In other words, if I fall short (sin), I may be either sympathetic to your sin and excuse it or be too hard on you because I hate my own weakness. Another way to look at this is if you are sick, I want to make you well because having been sick, too, I can identify with you. This may all look and sound good, but it leaves out God's will for our life. Because of this, Jesus did not judge or decide after what he saw or heard in the flesh; Jesus did what his heavenly Father told him to do. Jesus came to do the works of his Father. As Christians, finding and obeying God's will is one of the most difficult lessons that we are faced with learning. We must seek to know the mind of Christ.

I would like to put this into the perspective of salvation. When Smith Wigglesworth was in England, a woman of prestige came to one of his services. After having seen and heard him, the woman then sent for him the next day. She demanded that he pray for her because she was sick. Before praying for her, he asked that she first make certain alterations so that she would be "right with God." This sent the woman into an outrage. Mr. Wigglesworth did not back down; he told her that when she got right with God, she could meet him at the altar during one of his revival meetings. After a few days passed, the woman appeared at one of his meetings. It was during this meeting that God touched and healed her.

I sat down one evening with a man who was brought to me by two Christian brothers. The man was demon-possessed. After talking to him for a few minutes, I realized that he was in no way ready for salvation. The scripture tells us that when somebody comes, we are supposed to witness to him or her. It also says that we are supposed to have love and compassion for them. I looked straight at this man and said, "You could not care less about God, could you? You have absolutely no interest in Jesus Christ and getting salvation, do you?"

He said, "Yeah, you are right."

I then said, "Well, I am tired of wasting my time."

He replied, "I am tired of wasting my time too."

The two brothers who brought him were sitting there, looking dumbfounded, wondering what was wrong with me. I then said, "Sir, I am not going to waste your time and I am not going to waste any more of my time, but before you leave, I would like to pray for you."

He said, "Well, just a minute." He then paused and said, "The spirits say it is okay, so you can go ahead and pray for me."

I was not kidding when I said that he was demon-possessed; he talked to the demon spirits on a regular basis. I then reached over, laid my hand on his head, and said, "In the name of Jesus Christ, I bind the spirits that are blinding your mind and your eyes so that you cannot see the gospel of Jesus Christ. I pray that the power of the Holy Spirit will have reign over the spirits of darkness and bring you to a saving knowledge of Jesus Christ."

He sat there for a few minutes, totally stunned because the power of God touched him. I then told him that when he was ready to come to Christ to come to the church. He then left, and I did not expect to ever hear from him again. Six months later, he showed up at the church. He was then delivered, received Christ, received the Holy Spirit, and went on to become a dynamic Christian man. You see I could have coddled that man for six months and kept him from the place where God wanted to deal with him.

Our problem is that we take people off the cross instead of letting them die. The dead, not the ones who are playing opossum, shall hear my voice and be made alive. You must be dead in your sins and trespasses, pleading out for God's mercy before you can be made alive. This is the only way to salvation. Many people come before they get to that point, and they do not have a true conversion experience.

John 5:17–20 says:

> But Jesus answered them, My Father worketh hitherto,
> and I work. Therefore the Jews sought the more to kill him,

because he not only had broken the sabbath, but said also that God was his Father, making himself equal with God. Then answered Jesus and said unto them, Verily, verily, I say unto you, The Son can do nothing of himself, but what he seeth the Father do: for what things soever he doeth, these also doeth the Son likewise. For the Father loveth the Son, and showeth him all things that himself doeth: and he will show him greater works than these, that ye may marvel.

From the passages above, Jesus lays it all on the line and says that he cannot do anything unless his Father does it. Instead of this being a scary thing, it is an incredibly positive and powerful thing. I know I do not have the power to heal anybody. I know I cannot save anybody. The fact of the matter is that I cannot even convince anybody that they are lost and need to be saved. Only God can do this.

The beautiful thing is that we have a Father who can do it. This is exactly what Jesus knew. If we think back to when we were children, we thought that our dad was the biggest and best thing that ever lived; whatever he would do was so fascinating. As children, we were totally trusting in our father. Just think of how much greater our heavenly Father is with the things that he can do.

John 9:1–9 says:

And as Jesus passed by, he saw a man which was blind from his birth. And his disciples asked him, saying, Master, who did sin, this man, or his parents, that he was born blind? Jesus answered, Neither hath this man sinned, nor his parents: but that the works of God should be made manifest in him. I must work the works of him that sent me, while it is day: the night cometh, when no man can work. As long as I am in the world, I am the light of the world. When he had thus spoken, he spat on the ground, and made clay of the spittle, and he anointed the eyes of the blind man with the clay, and said unto him, Go, wash in the pool of Silo'am, (which is by interpretation, Sent.) He went his way therefore, and washed, and came seeing. The neighbors therefore, and they which before had seen him that he was blind, said, Is not this he that sat and begged? Some said, This is he: others said, He is like him: but he said, I am he.

John 8:26–38 says:

I have many things to say and to judge of you: but he that sent me is true; and I speak to the world those things which I have heard of him. They understood not that he spake to them of the Father. Then said Jesus unto them, When ye have lifted up the Son of man, then shall ye know that I am he, and that I do nothing of myself; but as my Father hath taught me, I speak these things. And he that sent me is with me: the Father hath not left me alone; for I do always those things that please him. As he spake these words, many believed on him. Then said Jesus to those Jews which believed on him, If ye continue in my word, then are ye my disciples indeed; and ye shall know the truth, and the truth shall make you free. They answered him, We be Abraham's seed, and were never in bondage to any man: how sayest thou, Ye shall be made free? Jesus answered them, Verily, verily, I say unto you, Whosoever committeth sin is the servant of sin. And the servant abideth not in the house for ever: but the Son abideth ever. If the Son therefore shall make you free, ye shall be free indeed. I know that ye are Abraham's seed; but ye seek to kill me, because my word hath no place in you. I speak that which I have seen with my Father: and ye do that which ye have seen with your father.

John 12:49–50 says:

For I have not spoken of myself; but the Father which sent me, he gave me a commandment, what I should say, and what I should speak. And I know that his commandment is life everlasting: whatsoever I speak therefore, even as the Father said unto me, so I speak.

John 14:7–12 says:

If ye had known me, ye should have known my Father also: and from henceforth ye know him, and have seen him. Philip saith unto him, Lord, show us the Father, and it sufficeth us. Jesus saith unto him, Have I been so long time with you, and yet hast thou not known me, Philip? he that hath seen me hath seen the Father; and how sayest thou then, Show us the Father? Believest thou not that I am in the Father, and the Father in me? the words that I speak unto you I speak not of myself: but the Father that dwelleth in me, he doeth the works. Believe me that I am in the Father, and the Father in me: or else believe me for the very works' sake. Verily, verily, I say unto you, He that believeth on me, the works that I do shall he do also; and greater works than these shall he do; because I go unto my Father.

The common message being expressed in all the passages above is that Jesus does only the works and speaks only the words that his Father has taught him. As living Christians, sometimes we fail to understand that to see his living Word, and to have it brought alive to us is to see Jesus. And to see Jesus is to see the Holy Father. In other words, Jesus is the image of his Father, and to see him is to see the Holy Father.

I have mentioned once before that this is the scripture that God gave to me after I accepted Christ, and these words were powerful to me. I believe that if God saved me, then all the Bible is true. I believe in his Word, even though I have not yet seen many of the things mentioned in it. The Lord walked on water; I have never walked on water. I have not seen the dead raised. I have seen people miraculously healed and demons come out of people. Also I have seen God speak with authority. I was thinking about this very thing the other day.

People have said that those in foreign counties have a need to see miracles, and that is why God is doing it there. They also say that in the US, we have doctors, hospitals, and the Word so abundantly clear to us that we do not need miracles. I then felt the Lord say to me, "What's wrong with you people? I need to manifest myself just as much in the US as I do in Africa, South America, and the Far East. I need and desire to be manifest, but my people have compromised themselves and have become so lukewarm that I am about to spew them out of my mouth."

God is looking for people who will commit themselves to trust him and walk with him in the same dedication that those in the foreign countries are doing. Our problem is that we have too many conveniences. I am just as guilty as anybody; when I come home at night, I am tired and exhausted. So I sit down and turn on the TV. I do it only intending on watching a little bit, but before I know it, it is time to go to bed. I could have been using the time in prayer or in studying the Word of God. I could have been seeking to hear from God. Then maybe I might be able to see the manifestations.

God has not quit manifesting himself in the United States of America because Satan certainly manifests himself. If Satan comes in like a flood, God will rise and stand against him if his people will pray and believe, but we do not do it. We want to go to church and be entertained with beautiful music. When are we going to call a prayer meeting and just pray with a broken heart and commitment? We are not going to until we fully realize that those who do not have Christ are going to go to hell.

Jesus has given us the example, but we just do not seem to want to come to that place because it requires commitment, dedication, and laying aside the trivial things that have become so important in our lives.

I feel that sometimes we have the whole total realm of spirituality mixed up. In other words, sometimes being in church might be the wrong place for us. Sometimes we are in such a hurry to get to church that we miss the person with the great need. For example, when they came to Jesus because the man's daughter was dying, and along the way someone touched the hem of his garment and was healed, Jesus stood there and took time to minister to her. In the meantime, the girl died.

Lord, if you had not of been so late, this girl would not have died. He was not too late to raise her from the dead. Do not misunderstand me. Most of the time, we need to be in church, but there are times when God says that your son, daughter, mother, brother, or neighbor needs somebody to love them. They may not understand church, but they understand love.

I came from a family where I was raised Methodist. When I met my wife, she was a Baptist, which was a no-no in the Methodist church. The problem was when I became a Baptist, I was not saved; I thought I was, but I was not. After I got saved, I was filled with the Spirit and became really filled with pride. My mother and father then came to visit. My mother needed healing severely; she had rheumatoid arthritis. I hit her full force with the fact that God could heal her because I had just seen a man with a severed spinal cord healed as well as other miracles.

In about three hours, I had done enough damage that it took about ten years to fix. My father took me aside and said, "If you don't shut up, we're leaving. Your mother has had all of this that she can handle."

Several years later, during the nasty, cold month of November, my mother called to tell me that my father was to receive an award, and they wanted me to come. Financially, I did not have the money, and the thought of packing up three small children and driving to North Dakota during winter did not really appeal to me. God then spoke to me and said, "You go. I will provide."

When we got to North Dakota, it was freezing cold. We were sitting outside in the stands of the football stadium with blowing winds, snow, and a chill factor of twenty below. We stayed until after the awards were given at halftime. It was the first time that I ever remember my dad hugging me. He hugged me and said, "Son, you'll never know how much this meant to me. I know how hard it was for you to get here, but you came, and I love you for it and appreciate it." Little did I know at that time that my dad did not know Jesus Christ as his Savior; my mother did. If you were to look at them both, you would have thought that it was the other way around.

A few years later, I sent some videotaped messages of my sermons to my dad. After my mother died, he accepted Christ. Those tapes played a big role in his salvation. He heard and listened because at times, when they needed things, we went, did the things they needed, and loved them. We must remember to never ever overlook love. Also, we must never put church over family while at the same time not allowing family to compromise church. If we talk to the Lord, he will guide us.

John 14:13–15 says:

And whatsoever ye shall ask in my name, that will I do, that the Father may be glorified in the Son. If ye shall ask any thing in my name, I will do it. If ye love me, keep my commandments.

Romans 8:9 says:

But ye are not in the flesh, but in the Spirit, if so be that the Spirit of God dwell in you. Now if any man have not the Spirit of Christ, he is none of his.

You can go out and spend a fortune buying books that tell you how to walk in the Spirit and how to be led by the Spirit or you can save your money and look at the passage above. You are in the Spirit if you have accepted Christ. The Spirit dwells in us, but we must learn to listen to him. Sometimes this means being quiet and just listening, and sometimes when he speaks, it means "act."

John 16:12–15 says:

I have yet many things to say unto you, but ye cannot bear them now. Howbeit when he, the Spirit of truth, is come, he will guide you into all truth: for he shall not speak of himself; but whatsoever he shall hear, that shall he speak: and he will show you things to come. He shall glorify me: for he shall receive of mine, and shall show it unto you. All things that the Father hath are mine: therefore said I, that he shall take of mine, and shall show it unto you.

In the passage above, God is saying that he is going to show the Holy Spirit the things that are happening, and then the Holy Spirit is going to show us. I was once in a situation where I was having to minister until three or four o'clock in the morning in order to reach everyone who was in need with the problem being that it took me at least forty-five minutes to find out what a person's need was.

Let us be honest, how many times when someone comes for prayer, do they really tell their actual needs? Sometimes people are superficial and are hoping that God does not show the sin in their life, which only serves to keep someone from praying for it and meeting the need.

I finally had to say, "Jesus, I don't have time to minister to all of these people because it is taking me too long." I then said to him, "Jesus, you are still in the world today, and you still perceive needs."

He said, "Yes, I am, and I am showing the Holy Spirit who would love to show you, if you would just listen."

I said, "I am ready, Lord."

So the next Monday night, I ministered in the Bible study. When I got through, a woman came up to me who had great needs. The Lord spoke to me and said, "I turned to the woman who was brought in adultery and said, 'Neither do I condemn you. Go and sin no more.'"

I then turned to this woman, who I had never seen before, and restated what the Lord had just said to me, saying, "Jesus said to the woman caught in adultery and brought to Him, 'Neither do I condemn you. Go and sin no more.'"

The woman then fell to the floor, crying, and grabbed me by the legs, saying, "Thank you. Thank you."

I said to her, "What do you mean?"

She said, "I am a prostitute and I did not think that God could forgive me." She was delivered from demon-possession, prayed, received Christ, and was filled with the Holy Spirit. This all happened within a period of seven to ten minutes.

The message I am trying to convey is that it is bold and blunt to turn to someone and say, "Go and sin no more." However, when God goes before you, Jesus perceives the need, and they are just waiting to hear the truth.

I'm going to tell this story because I feel that it most clearly illustrates how the Lord works. One day, I received a phone call from my barber, saying that he was in excruciating pain. He said that he couldn't sit down, lie down, nor walk around without his neck "killing" him. The Lord spoke to me, telling me to lay hands on him, and he would heal him. So I went over to his house and prayed for him, and he was healed.

The way that this happened was that when he called me, the Lord spoke to me, giving me a scripture. This is how God speaks to you; faith comes by hearing, and hearing by the Word. When you hear the Word, you hear faith. The Lord said to me very clearly, "You shall lay hands on the sick, and they shall recover." So I had to go to his house; I could not do it over the phone.

I asked him where he lived, and then I went over to his house. When I walked into his house, the Lord gave me another scripture. Jesus was standing at the grave of Lazarus, and he said, "Father, I know whatever I ask you, you are going to do, but that they may know, Lazarus come forth."

When I walked into that house, the Lord told me that he had healed him and that I must lay hands on him so that he would know that he had healed him. When I walked over and put my hands on his neck, I said, "So that you might know, I am asking that the power of the Holy Spirit flow through you, touch you, and heal you in the name of Jesus." After which, this man started jumping up and down, threw his hands in the air, and started praising God; he was healed.

At the time, I didn't know what had happened to his neck but later found out that he was born with one missing and one deformed vertebra in his neck. He went back to the doctor, who then x-rayed his neck, and found that he had perfect vertebras. God not only made him well, but he remade him.

If we will take the time and be patient, God will teach us, the Holy Spirit will direct us, and we will be able to walk in the Spirit and see the power of God.

The big thing is when someone comes and wants to be prayed for but does not have the faith or does not believe, then do not pray for healing unless God has spoken it to you. Instead, pray for God's grace until he gives you the understanding to know what to do; this way, you build faith instead of destroying it. You still have the same compassion, but you are not destroying faith by praying and having nothing happen. When we hear God's voice and act on it, God will be glorified. The miracle-working God will be manifested for his glory.

One of the biggest problems in receiving healing is that people are seeking the healing instead of seeking the healer. If we will seek the healer, we will get the mind of Christ and realize that God is sovereign. His main goal is to mold us into the image of his Son Jesus Christ.

# ABOUT THE AUTHOR

Dr. Ernest S. Martin grew up on a large ranch in North Dakota where his family had a dairy and also raised both commercial and registered Herefords. They grew wheat, durum, barley, oats, and alfalfa hay. Growing up on a farm and ranch gave Ernest insight into the Scriptures as many illustrations in the Word of God are related to sheep, goats, and growing grain.

While in high school, Ernest studied a curriculum geared to be an engineer but changed to veterinary medicine at North Dakota State University. He received his DVM from Oklahoma State University. While doing post-doctoral research at OSU, he met his wife, Jan, who was doing graduate work in chemistry. They were married eleven weeks later in 1966.

After moving to Dallas, Texas, Ernest eventually had his own animal hospital. He received Jesus as his Savior on August 21, 1970, and soon started an outreach Bible study for hippies. This outreach became a church which Ernest pastored while still practicing veterinary medicine. After selling his veterinary practice at age sixty-two, he went to firefighter school and became a volunteer firefighter, and he is currently the chaplain of the Melissa Fire Department. Ernest and his wife, Jan, have four sons, five granddaughters, and one grandson.